52 SECRETS TO BEING THE BEST EMPLOYEE EVER!

An Insider's Guide to Unlimited Career Success

BONNIE COX

Foreword by Roger Dawson

Cover design, layout, and editorial by Lori Weathers.

POWER TRAINING INSTITUTE

Power Training Institute
3820 State Street
Santa Barbara, CA 93105
866-456-TRAIN
www.powertraining.biz

ISBN 0-9772914-0-5

Copies of *52 Secrets to Being the Best Employee Ever* are available through Power Training Institute.

TABLE OF CONTENTS

FOREWORD

Finally! A book about developing good work habits and being a great employee – presented in an easy-to-manage and fun-to-practice format! *52 Secrets to Being The Best Employee Ever!* is a great read for every citizen of Corporate America – from the CEO on down.

Bonnie Cox' engaging lessons, complete with compelling personal stories and relevant anecdotes, reflect her firm belief in – and strong enthusiasm for – the ideals she espouses. With nearly 20 years of experience in human resources and career development, she has gained insight into jobs at every level in an organization – as well as the personal and interpersonal skills needed to move upward at a company.

Ms. Cox' lessons are valuable as a whole, but their true merit lies in the way they are presented. Each lesson begins with a mandate for the week – an Attitude of Excellence, as she calls it – that serves as the starter pistol on your race down the path to career success. Ms. Cox' concepts and ideas will fuel your sprint toward becoming a more valuable member of your corporate team and that likely means a more highly rewarded one. Also, her thought-provoking questions and journal opportunities allow for meaningful reflection about how you performed as you worked your way toward the finish line.

This book provides the tools every employee needs to improve their personal and interpersonal skills, and every reader will come away feeling like they have already achieved a measure of career success. How rewarding it will be as you look back over your journey to becoming the Best Employee Ever!

Roger Dawson, President and CEO of Power Negotiating Institute, is the author of Secrets of Power Negotiating. *His next book, due in the spring of 2006 from Career Press, is* Secrets of Power Salary Negotiating.

INTRODUCTION

Why is it that some of the most brilliant, talented, and educated people have so many failures in their jobs? Why do they move from place to place, continually looking for that perfect opportunity – or worse, hunker down in a job they hate and waste years making only a fraction of the contribution (and receiving only a fraction of the reward) of which they are capable?

THE PROBLEM

Career failure happens when we don't possess the basic skills we need for success. Sure, we're all a product of our heredity and environment. Unfortunately, some of us weren't as fortunate as others to have good parenting or schooling, nor did we receive adequate, proper socialization. Career stagnation happens when we possess some basic skills for success but not enough to feel truly successful.

Whatever the reason, we have been saddled with self-defeating beliefs that cause us to behave in self-sabotaging ways. Conversely, corporations are looking for employees who are reliable, consistent, productive, supportive, and who can get along well with others.

A corporation's culture is a collection of values, beliefs, norms, and customs that govern the workplace. The problem is, not all employees "buy into" or identify with their organization's culture. Conflicts arise when there is a misalignment between the employee's values and those of the organization. This book is for those employees.

THE SOLUTION

52 Secrets to Being the Best Employee Ever! is a practical how-to book for employees and managers alike. It is a collection of proven workplace principles that have helped many people find career success. These principles represent attitudes and behaviors that, if applied correctly and consistently, will have a positive impact on an organization's corporate culture.

These secrets are important tools because organizations are looking for employees who believe in and accept the company's goals and values. They want employees who are willing to make a commitment and exert effort on the company's behalf. The goal of this book is to create a positive, momentous affect on attitudes, beliefs, and cultures. These principles will give employees the skills and attitudes they need to make a strong organizational commitment – and to impact their company from the inside out.

AN OVERVIEW

This book has been designed to help you develop positive attitudes and skills in two major areas: individually and interpersonally.

Part 1 of the book is dedicated to helping you develop the internal attitudes and beliefs necessary for career success. It will show you how a change of attitude always starts on the inside. And only if you have the right attitude will you begin to demonstrate the right behaviors. This section will help you get below the surface and see why it is in your best interest to embrace certain beliefs.

Part 2 is focused on helping you develop the skills to interact successfully with work colleagues. It covers such things as communication, building relationships, and creating a positive working environment. It is your ability to get along with others, be supportive of your boss and co-workers, and resolve conflict that will prove to be the most critical skills for your success.

This book is presented in weekly lessons. Each lesson begins with the Attitude of Excellence necessary for success. The CONCEPT section explains the ideas behind the Attitude of Excellence, and the APPLICATION offers ideas or assignments to apply during the week. Finally, the EVALUATE & JOURNAL section is designed to have you reflect on your week. It includes a handful of reflective questions to think about as you make your journal entry in the space provided.

You may start your journey through this book at any time of the year. Take your time with the lessons. Don't skip ahead or read it all at once. The more time you spend on each weekly lesson, the more you will begin to embody these principles. So, carefully reflect on and practice each one.

The suggestions in this book are based on years of practical, in-the-trenches experiences of being an employee, managing employees, and coaching employees. The important thing to remember is that these principles are designed to change you and your attitudes. This is not about how these changes will affect others. It is about how these changes will affect you and help you achieve career success. And, if you happen to impress your bosses in the meantime, all the better!

Finally, if you experience any great success stories as a result of implementing these principles, I'd like to hear about them! Please feel free to e-mail them to me at register@powertraining.biz.

Thank you for your hard work and for sticking with it! Please accept my personal best wishes for a happy and successful career.

WORKING ON ME:

PERSONAL SKILLS FOR SUCCESS

Realize That Your Attitude Is Everything!

CONCEPT

An attitude is simply a state of mind. A way of looking at things (life, others, ourselves). The power of attitude, however, is how it affects our actions. Everything we say and everything we do is a direct result of our attitude. My dad once said, "Give me someone with a positive attitude, and I can teach them to do anything."

We once hired a young woman who was working on her master's degree but who agreed to be our receptionist on a part-time basis. Many people had previously occupied that position, and generally, the attitude was one of "I can do better than this" or "I'm only doing this until I find something better." The thing that was so remarkable about this woman, however, was her positive attitude. She was not only thankful for the job while she pursued her studies, but she used the position to learn everything she could about the operations of our company! She offered to help Human Resources do data entry and thereby learned our software program. She offered to help Accounting process employment verification requests and thereby learned the whole legal process of garnishments, credit reports, and reference checking. Eventually, she became so valuable that she was offered a full-time position in the company. It was her attitude that helped her be successful in everything she did.

I like what motivational speaker Zig Ziglar recommends: do a "checkup from the neck up" and get rid of that "stinkin' thinkin'!" [1] When we get rid of our negative attitudes, we actually get excited and enthusiastic about life. We no longer focus on "fair" or "better." We focus on what we can learn and how we change our lives.

I saw first-hand how a change in attitude can change a person's life. When Dr. Norman Vincent Peale first published his book *The Power of Positive Thinking,* someone gave a copy of it to my mother. She had struggled with depression for years. But the words of this book were like salve on an open wound. Nothing in her life changed, but her perception of reality did. She was able to find contentment in her circumstances, even though nothing had really changed.

Yes, we want a positive mental attitude because it makes others want to be around us. But we need a positive mental attitude because of what it does for us. It allows us to see things differently. We can see opportunity instead of discouragement. It changes our glass from half empty to half full. And it opens up a whole new world. Employers want employees with a positive attitude. And they're willing to create opportunities for them.

APPLICATION

This week, refuse to complain about anything. Instead, decide to look at things differently … more positively. Find at least one spot of good in any bad situation. Continually ask yourself, "What can I learn from this? How can this situation make me a better person/employee?" Stay objective. Think about which attitude will get you the best results over time. Will you find more contentment with a negative attitude or a positive one? The choice is yours.

EVALUATE & JOURNAL

On Friday, think about the following questions as you prepare to journal.

1. Record at least one incident where you were able to find the good instead of dwelling on the bad. How difficult was it for you? What made it easier?

2. How did being positive affect your feelings about the situation in which you found yourself? How did it affect your actions?

3. Did you find that people treated you differently when you demonstrated a positive attitude? How did your positive attitude affect your interpersonal relationships?

4. Was it difficult to not complain? How did you catch yourself before voicing a complaint?

5. What did you learn about the power of positive thinking? What can you do to keep this new attitude going into next week? And the week after that?

_____

_____

_____

_____

_____

_____

_____

_____

_____

_____

_____

_____

_____

_____

_____

_____

_____

_____

_____

Learn Everything You Can about Your "Blindside."

CONCEPT

Did you know you have a blindside [2] – things about yourself that others can see … but you can't? Well, we all have one. Our goal, then, should be to solicit enough feedback so we can change the self-sabotaging behaviors that reside there. But we won't unless we see it as an opportunity to improve.

I once worked with a woman who had a reputation for being cold and aloof. After getting to know her, I realized that she was simply shy and socially awkward. In her effort to protect herself, she came across as unfriendly and judgmental.

One of the ways we can learn about our blindside is through feedback (usually in the form of criticism and correction). We may not like criticism, but it does give us insight. If we can remain open and ask enough questions, we can find wonderful hidden nuggets of truth about ourselves in criticism. Likewise, being corrected is not fun, but think of it like pruning a fruit tree. If a fruit tree is not pruned, it will not bear fruit the next year. Isn't that similar to us? We can't grow without correction.

The final way we can learn about our blindside is by using what author Stephen Covey calls the social mirror [3] (or others' reactions to our behavior). You know how we don't like it when people brag or whine about themselves? Well, we try to send subtle messages to them with our behavior. We may scowl or frown to show our disapproval. Or we may raise an eyebrow in skepticism. But what we are trying to do is communicate through our nonverbal signals that we think the person is a self-absorbed bore.

Other people send us those types of messages when they disapprove of our behavior. So, their reactions are like a mirror that helps reflect their hidden feelings about us. We need to be tuned in to these nonverbal clues so we can know how we're being perceived – then modify our self-sabotaging behavior accordingly.

So, ready? Chin up. Eyes and heart open. Start noticing the social mirror. You'll be amazed at what you see there!

APPLICATION

This week, start looking for insights into your blindside. Notice how people respond to you. What do their words and body language tell you? If they were reacting to someone else in the same manner, what kinds of conclusions would you draw about the person? Before the end of the week, ask at least two people for honest feedback (about your work, your personality, your interactions with others, etc.).

EVALUATE & JOURNAL

On Friday, think about the following questions as you prepare to journal.

1. What did you learn about yourself this week?

2. How difficult was it to intentionally seek feedback about yourself? Did you become defensive, or were you able to "take it on the chin?"

3. How will you use this information to improve your interactions with others? What will you be willing to do to make changes in your behavior?

4. Now, journal what you have learned.

_____

_____

_____

_____

_____

_____

_____

_____

_____

_____

_____

_____

_____

_____

_____

_____

_____

_____

_____

_____

_____

_____

Know Your Strengths. Understand Your Weaknesses.

CONCEPT

Everyone has strengths and weaknesses. Things that serve us and our employers well – and things that detract from our performance. Our goal should be to maximize our strengths and minimize our weaknesses.

First, let's consider strengths. Think about what you do well. In what areas do you receive the most compliments? What kinds of things come easy to you? What do you enjoy doing? Look for ways to alter your job slightly so you are doing more of what you do well. Find your successes and build on them.

Now, let's consider weaknesses. Weaknesses are not necessarily bad. We all have them. In fact, let's rephrase our thinking and consider weaknesses as opportunities for growth and improvement. The trick is to find a way to make them less pronounced. So, think about areas in your life that are not going well. Where are you stuck? What is holding you back? What are your limitations? Find your weaknesses and set about to correct them. Ask for help. Remember, asking for help is not a sign of weakness but of strength.

APPLICATION

This week, make a list of your strengths, and use them every opportunity you get. Likewise, make a list of your weaknesses. Come up with one specific and concrete way you can begin to overcome that limitation. Identify someone who has strengths in one of your weak areas. Make a point of asking that person for help.

EVALUATE & JOURNAL

On Friday, think about the following questions as you prepare to journal.

1. What are some of your strengths? How have they helped you be successful in your job so far? How could you find opportunities to use them more often?

2. What are some of your weaknesses? Were you able to find someone who has strength in those areas and who can coach you? How will that help you?

3. How did it feel to ask for help? Humbling? Empowering? Did you find some ways to improve?

4. Now, journal what you have learned.

_____

_____

_____

_____

_____

_____

_____

_____

_____

_____

_____

_____

_____

_____

_____

_____

_____

_____

_____

_____

_____

_____

_____

_____

Guard Your Own Self-Image.

CONCEPT

Who is your biggest critic? Is it you? If so, you're not alone. Unfortunately, we tend to be harder on ourselves than others are. It is crucially important that we love and approve of ourselves and that we learn to forgive ourselves for our mistakes.

I had to learn this lesson the hard way. I grew up on a large farm in northern Minnesota. We weren't poor, but we weren't rich either. We were a great family with supportive parents and siblings. However, from my earliest memories, I remember feeling inferior to those who lived "in town." Somehow, I began to believe that people from rural areas were inferior to those from the city. For a time, this negative self-image presented me with limitation after limitation. One day, I read some advice about "never despising humble beginnings." As I continued my education, I began to realize that many famous and successful people had, indeed, gotten their start in rural areas and on farms. It was the permission I needed to get past this archaic and limiting belief and finally move on.

So, let me share some of the lessons I've learned along the way:

- Your self-esteem is all you have. First Lady Eleanor Roosevelt once said, "Nobody can make you feel inferior without your consent."
- Don't try to be perfect. No one is. Just do your best.
- Get up after you fall. When you fail, see it as an opportunity to learn something new.
- Don't compare yourself to others. John Wooden, the UCLA basketball coach, always encouraged his players to be the best they could be, rather than trying to be better than someone else.
- Check your ego at the door.
- Keep your insecurities to yourself and don't overcompensate for them.
- Don't take yourself too seriously. Stay humble. Learn to laugh at yourself. Keep things in perspective.
- Treat yourself well. Repeat encouraging self-affirmations every day.

APPLICATION

This week, write at least three positive affirmations about yourself. (Start each one with "I am …"). Paste them on your bathroom mirror and read them aloud every morning. Give yourself some slack. Find ways to compliment yourself. At least once this week, look in the mirror and say, "I love you, and I accept you just the way you are."

EVALUATE & JOURNAL

On Friday, think about the following questions as you prepare to journal.

1. What limiting and self-sabotaging beliefs did you discover you have? How did you put them in perspective?

2. Write out your three affirmations. How did repeating the affirmations every day help you strengthen your self-image?

3. What did you learn from this experience? Who do you know who could give you some additional pointers? Connect with them.

_____

_____

_____

_____

_____

_____

_____

_____

_____

_____

_____

_____

_____

_____

_____

_____

_____

_____

_____

_____

_____

Think Like a Business Owner.

CONCEPT

Do you want to enjoy unlimited success in your career? The best piece of advice anywhere is to "think like a business owner," to see the world from an owner's perspective.

Imagine taking all of your savings, mortgaging your house, and signing on for long-term debt to rent a space, purchase equipment, and hire employees. Remember, you're a small business owner without the expertise of a CFO, Human Resources expert, or Quality Control manager. You're all on your own, trying to navigate the murky waters of regulations and competition – and survive in your new venture. Scary, huh?

Now imagine the kind of employee you'd want working for you. Would you rather have a clock-watcher who takes every second of their break and who continually asks for more and more perks? Or would you want a dedicated, hard-working employee who understands and supports your vision for a successful future?

If you can see life through a business owner's eyes, you'll see hope and uncertainty, fear and promise. You'll also see many opportunities to create incredible value for yourself.

We once had the good fortune to hire such an employee in our small business. Ali had incredible insights and emotional maturity. She seemed to instinctively know what needed to be done to get our new business off the ground. She empathized with our struggles and worries. Turns out, she was absolutely invaluable to the success of our business. Although we could barely afford to do so, we paid her like royalty. And she was worth every penny!

So, think like a business owner. Walk a mile in their shoes. Feel the stress. Anticipate the fear. Then, perform accordingly.

APPLICATION

This week, look for opportunities to take an owner's perspective. Specifically look in any areas that can increase revenue, decrease costs, or increase productivity. Then, ask yourself, "How would I view this situation differently if it were my checking account on the line?" How did you enjoy the view?

EVALUATE & JOURNAL

On Friday, think about the following questions as you prepare to journal.

1. How difficult was it to imagine things from an owner's perspective? Why do you think that is?

2. Do you know anyone who "thinks like a business owner" quite naturally? How has it affected that person's career success over time?

3. What is the lesson to be learned here? How can you use it to increase your effectiveness in your job?

4. Now, journal what you have learned. Record any insights you have gained.

_____

_____

_____

_____

_____

_____

_____

_____

_____

_____

_____

_____

_____

_____

_____

_____

_____

_____

_____

Love Your Job – Or Leave It.

CONCEPT

Chinese philosopher Confucius once said: Choose a job you love, and you'll never have to work another day in your life." Other authors call it passion, commitment, or dedication. Whatever you want to call it, the message is clear. You must either love your job ... or you must leave it.

Many people get disgruntled in their jobs. They don't like the work. They don't like the pay. They don't like their boss. Guess what? They might think it's a secret, but everybody already knows how they feel. In fact, these attitudes can actually become self-limiting! Why? Because attitudes drive actions. So, instead of doing more than expected, they do less. Instead of supporting the company, they tear it down. Then, their actual attitude and slacking performance puts them in jeopardy of losing their job.

The lesson here is, if you don't like your job, don't waste your own (and everyone else's) time. If you can't support the company's culture, customs, or goals, you shouldn't be there. Oh, sure, your boss will make mistakes. That's only human. But you must find a way to support that boss regardless. That means making the boss look good, speaking well of the team, and giving your constant support to the organization (who is signing your paycheck, by the way). You'll be happier and so will everyone else.

Remember, there is no shame in pursuing what you love to do. But, you cannot move on to new and better situations when you are stuck in ones you don't like. So, find out what you love to do. Then, go find a company who will pay you for it.

APPLICATION

This week, take a hard, objective look at yourself. Look at your work performance. Are you performing above or below expectations? How about your dedication to the company? Do you speak highly of your boss and team? If you find that you don't love your job, you really only have two choices: change your attitude or change your job. What will you do?

EVALUATE & JOURNAL

On Friday, think about the following questions as you prepare to journal.

1. How did you rate your work performance? Above or below average?

2. If you were your boss, would you be satisfied with your attitude and performance?

3. Now, what if you owned your company? Would you want all of your employees to have attitudes and performance at your level? If yes, congratulations! Keep up the good work! It'll lead to your success. If no, it's time to move on. What steps will you take to make that happen?

4. Now, journal what you have learned. Record any insights you have gained.

_____

_____

_____

_____

_____

_____

_____

_____

_____

_____

_____

_____

_____

_____

_____

_____

_____

_____

_____

_____

_____

_____

_____

Always Accept Personal Responsibility.

CONCEPT

It is called "personal responsibility" because it starts with me. And you. It means we stand by our decisions and actions, good or bad.

When we accept personal responsibility, we can no longer play the blame game. We can no longer be victims. There are no excuses, no scapegoats. We have to own our decisions. And actions. And consequences.

A little friend of mine, Max, would come home from kindergarten every day, and his mother would ask him what he learned that day. Then, she would do some Q&A exercises with him to reinforce his learning. He must have gotten tired of the routine, because one day when he came home, he put his little hands on his hips and announced to his mother, "They didn't teach me anything new today … but I put in my time." Great example of what "they" didn't do. But how many adults do you know who have similar complaints? "They didn't train me," or "They haven't given me an opportunity."

The point is, when we don't accept responsibility for our own actions (or lack of), we lose personal power. We actually become self-destructive and unreliable. But if we do accept this responsibility, it increases our integrity. People learn to trust us. The world opens up to us. We gain more and more responsibility. It takes us to the top. People say, "Now, there's someone who can make things happen."

APPLICATION

This week, refuse to blame others. Never ask questions that begin with "why" or "who" (as in, "who messed up this time?") [4] Instead, step to the plate, and be responsible. Look for opportunities to ask questions that begin with "how" or "what" (for example, "What can I do to get the training I need?"). Take ownership of everything you do: phone calls, interactions, promises, deadlines, goals, wins, losses … everything. Leave people with the impression that you are accountable, responsible, and empowered.

EVALUATE & JOURNAL

On Friday, think about the following questions as you prepare to journal.

1. How did it feel to take 100% responsibility for everything you said and did this week? Why?

2. How do you think accepting personal responsibility could help you be more successful over time?

3. Identify at least one person who exemplifies personal accountability. What do they do? What can you learn from them?

4. Now, journal what you have learned. Record any insights you have gained.

_____

_____

_____

_____

_____

_____

_____

_____

_____

_____

_____

_____

_____

_____

_____

_____

_____

_____

_____

_____

_____

_____

_____

Have a Strategic Plan for Your Life.

CONCEPT

Musician John Lennon once said, "Life is what happens while you're busy making other plans." That's certainly how life happened for me. I didn't have a plan. It just sort of happened. Because I happened to be in the right place at the right time, job opportunities opened up for me. But it certainly wasn't because I had a plan.

I wish now that I had spent more time early on deciding where I wanted to go, what I wanted to do. Some people know from the time they are five years old that they want to be a teacher or a scientist. I never knew what I wanted to be, so I delayed making important decisions about my career until later in life. It's not that I'm unhappy with my life. I'm not. But it would have been quite different, I'm sure, if I'd had a plan.

If I had it to do over, here's what I'd do:

- Take time to define my values, my goals, and myself. What do I stand for? What do I believe in? Where and who do I want to be?
- Make yearly, monthly, and weekly goals. Write them down. If it isn't written down, it didn't happen (and it's not going to happen).
- Break goals into objectives and put them on a timeline. Accomplish small things ... continually.
- Learn to "invest" my time ... not just spend it. Time is such a limited commodity and, once spent, we can't get it back.
- Start somewhere ... anywhere ... just start! And the sooner the better.

When I finally (sort of) figured it out, I was in my 50s. That's when I decided to go back to school and get my master's degree. I thought about what 20th-century radio personality and philosopher Earl Nightingale once said, "The time will pass anyway; you might just as well put that passing time to the best possible use." So, remember, it's never too late! Just start!

APPLICATION

This week, think about your life and your goals. Where do you want to be in 15 years? Who do you want to be? Tomorrow is just a collection of yesterdays. What will you start doing today that could change all of your tomorrows? Set a goal to improve in at least one area every day. Find someone who can coach you through this process. It's not difficult, but you need someone who can hold you accountable. Who could that be?

EVALUATE & JOURNAL

On Friday, think about the following questions as you prepare to journal.

1. Journal for two minutes about where you'd like your life to be in 15 years.

2. What do you need to do to ensure you reach that goal? What are the first and second steps you need to take?

3. How will you set your plan in motion? What will you do, starting today?

Approach Life with a Sense of Urgency.

CONCEPT

The most consistently successful people I know all have an incredible sense of urgency about everything they do. They know where they're going, and they can't wait to get there. They are focused on their goals with laser-beam precision. Nothing gets them off-track. Their philosophy is, "Why would you want to put off until tomorrow what you can get done today? Besides, tomorrow will have new challenges!"

How do we develop this sense of urgency, this *fire in the belly*? By having a sense of purpose. Having a passion about what we do. Having things we want and need to accomplish. Then singularly focusing all our energies in that area.

I'm reminded of a saying by Samuel Johnson, an 18th-century author and poet: "Nothing concentrates the mind like the imminent prospect of a hanging." Interesting, isn't it? If we knew we were going to die in the morning, we'd stay up all night thinking about what we needed to do to make sure our lives counted for something. We'd feel a real sense of urgency. So, the message is clear. As Mohandas Gandhi said, "you must live as if you were going to die tomorrow."

So, let's take a cue from some of the highly successful people we know – achievers who have a clear and focused singularity of purpose, to which everything else is subordinated.

APPLICATION

This week, find something in your job about which you can get excited – a project, a task, something you can sink your teeth into. If you can't think of one, ask your boss. Once you have the project, come up with a plan. Establish some self-imposed deadlines. Get started. Just take the first step. Hurry … time is flying by! I'm confident you will be surprised by the amount of energy and self-esteem you will generate by being urgently focused on achieving your goal.

EVALUATE & JOURNAL

On Friday, think about the following questions as you prepare to journal.

1. Describe the project you selected. What are the objectives and the deadlines you've established?

2. What did you do to get "into" the project? What kind of story did you tell yourself to generate excitement for the results?

3. How could you apply these techniques to other aspects of your job?

4. How do you think being passionate about your job could affect your career success?

CONCEPT

Early in my career, I wrote an article about office efficiency and entered it into a secretarial contest. Very unexpectedly, I placed second in the nation and won a "Secretary of the Year" scholarship award. The local paper even came by to take my picture and then wrote a short article. Obviously, I was very thankful for the money, which I used to continue my education. What I learned from this experience, however, is that not everyone was happy for me. Only one of the other secretaries even acknowledged my accomplishment and congratulated me. Why? Well, we could speculate, I suppose, but to what good end?

The first lesson I learned from this experience is to be thankful for everything that comes your way. Be content with what you have. Can't think of anything? Well, be grateful that you have a job and live in a country where disease and mortality rates are low. Get past any feelings of being "entitled." No one is entitled to anything. It is what we make it.

Second, learn to be happy for others. Be grateful when others have good fortune. Stay as far away from jealousy and covetousness as you can. Why? Not because it hurts the other person but because it hurts you. Who loses? You do. Again, I think John Wooden, UCLA coach had the right idea. He said that if you compare yourself to others, there will always be someone faster, taller, smarter, more handsome, or more beautiful. If we focus on what others have, we'll never be content. Instead, it's healthier to focus on our own attitude of gratitude. Trust me, those feelings – whether of jealousy or gratitude – may start on the inside, but they always show up on the outside … in everything we say and do.

APPLICATION

This week, make a list of at least 10 things for which you are grateful. If you find more than that, keep going! Now, think of someone with whom you work, perhaps someone you do not particularly like, and record at least three positive things about that person. Next, think of some blessings they have in their life (their family, their position, their health, their education, etc.). Say to yourself, "I'm really genuinely happy for them that they have [fill in the blank.]" It is not about what that statement does for them … but what it does for you. It is very liberating to give up feelings of jealousy and replace them with feelings of gratitude.

EVALUATE & JOURNAL

On Friday, think about the following questions as you prepare to journal.

1. How many things could you list for which you were grateful? Did you find that there were more than you could possibly list? How did it change your attitude about "fairness" issues and "entitlements?"

2. Describe your initial feelings when you were asked to think of positive things about someone you disliked? Was there some pain? Or did you begin to feel some freedom in acknowledging their good fortune?

3. How did making a list of their positive attributes help you overcome your negative feelings about that person? If not, why not?

4. What did you learn from this lesson? How did it change you? How will it help you in the future when someone has good fortune?

_____

_____

_____

_____

_____

_____

_____

_____

_____

_____

_____

_____

_____

_____

_____

_____

_____

_____

_____

_____

_____

_____

Learn to Control Your Emotions.

CONCEPT

How many times have you seen someone fly off the handle and say things they later regret? Why does this happen? Because they are being led by their emotions and not their logic. See, when another person gets too close to discovering our hidden insecurities, feelings of inferiority, or fears, we become defensive and overreact. Our emotions take control – instead of our intellect or common sense.

For example, let's say that you have a fear of being insignificant. You will likely react the next time someone seemingly disregards or disrespects what you say or do. Your fear of feeling insignificant is triggered, and you will respond with fight (confrontation) or flight (avoidance).

Unless we can learn to control our emotions and our instinct to fight or flight, we will say or do things that create unpleasant – and embarrassing – consequences.

So, what is the answer? First, find out what triggers your emotions. Second, when you see that trigger coming, be aware that you might overreact. Stay in control by asking yourself, "What is it about what this person is saying or doing that is causing me to react?" Third, excuse yourself *before* you react. Think it through. You may still want to confront the person, but do it later when your emotions are under control.

Here are some other tricks that have worked well for others:

- Think about the big picture and keep things in perspective. Is this incident something with lasting effect? Learn to ask questions like, "So what? Who cares? What of it?"
- Get over things quickly. Don't waste your time and energy on things you can't change.
- Realize that most people do things for their own reasons. It's not about you. It's usually their own deal. They don't mean to upset you. So, don't let them.
- Focus on tolerance. Learn to overlook the little indiscretions of others.
- Don't hang on to it. There's a saying that no one is closer to you than someone you can't forgive. So, forgive … and forget about it.
- Learn from your mistakes. Everyone makes poor decisions now and then. But you have a choice. You can either learn from it and go on … or continue repeating the same self-sabotaging behavior.

APPLICATION

This week, look for patterns in your emotions. What kinds of things "hook" your emotions? Then, look for the underlying cause. When you feel attacked, think first. Is it really about you? Or is someone else just trying to get their needs met? Look for opportunities to reframe your feelings into something more positive and empowering.

EVALUATE & JOURNAL

On Friday, think about the following questions as you prepare to journal.

1. What did you learn about your emotions? What kinds of fears cause you to react?

2. Now that you know what triggers you emotionally, what will you do differently? Come up with your own plan of escape.

3. Identify those colleagues who can control their emotions. Ask them to give you some pointers.

4. Now, journal what you have learned.

_____

_____

_____

_____

_____

_____

_____

_____

_____

_____

_____

_____

_____

_____

_____

_____

_____

_____

_____

_____

_____

_____

Keep Your Support System Strong.

CONCEPT

Life is like a boxing match. We all need people who love and support us in our little corner of the ring. Who is that for you? A spouse? A friend? A family member? Whoever it is, remember that they are a critical component of your emotional and physical well-being.

One day, after a misunderstanding with my boss, I came home and collapsed in a heap. It all seemed so overwhelming. How could one have a fight with a boss and still have a job? How could I go back and face the situation again tomorrow? Left to my own devices, I would have stewed on the problem all night long. I would have recalled stories about other injustices until I had worked myself into a real state of mind.

Fortunately, my husband had a way of helping me put things in perspective. He said things like, "How bad can it really be? In the big scheme of things, this is probably just a little hiccup. In fact, he's probably forgotten all about it, given the pressures he is facing." When I would hear nothing of it, he reminded me, "Remember, you were looking for a job when you found this one. If this doesn't work out, you still have other options." Whew. I remember thinking, "Yeah, maybe it's not that bad. We'll talk about it in the morning. Worst-case scenario, I'll be looking for another job tomorrow afternoon. Best case, we'll clear the air, and everything will be back to normal." Sure enough, we had a talk, cleared the air, and things indeed went back to normal. In fact, I ended up working for that guy for another four years!

The point is, we need others to keep us balanced and keep things in perspective. Usually, nothing is as bad as we think it is. We just need someone to continue reminding us of that and to help us keep an open mind.

Here are some other ways you can keep your support system strong:

- Stay balanced. Don't spend too much time or energy in any one area of your life.
- Stay rested. Sleep is what recharges your batteries and clears your mind.
- Have some alone time every day. Use the time to reflect – on the past, the present, and the future. What needs "tweaking?"
- Relax. Focus on the big picture. In the long run, a lot of the little things don't really matter.
- Let your sick time accrue! You never know, you may really need it someday!

APPLICATION

This week, list the people in your support system. Next, make sure to let them know how important they are to you. If you need more support, immediately start cultivating friends on whom you can count. Take a critical look at where you spend your time. Are you out of whack in any area? Do you spend too much time at work? Or not enough? Are you exercising your body and your mind? Are you getting enough rest? If not, make some changes to your schedule.

EVALUATE & JOURNAL

On Friday, think about the following questions as you prepare to journal.

1. List the supporters in your corner of the boxing ring. How have they helped you in the past?

2. Did you let everyone in your support system know how important they are to you? How did they react? How did it strengthen your relationship?

3. What else did you discover about your support system? Are you eating right? Exercising? Getting enough rest? What changes did you decide to make to your schedule?

4. What commitment will you make for the future? How will you make sure that you have a consistently strong support system?

_____

_____

_____

_____

_____

_____

_____

_____

_____

_____

_____

_____

_____

_____

_____

_____

_____

_____

_____

_____

CONCEPT

Work, along with many other things we do in life, has become the center of our existence. Whether we're feeling pressure to meet an important deadline or simply to do more in less time, we feel the stress. Either way, there is very little time at the beginning or the end of the day to focus on our health. Or so it seems.

But even if we are busy and can't leave our offices on time, there are several things we can do to rejuvenate our energies. For example, take one minute sometime during the day to relax. Close your eyes and think about the most peaceful and safe place you have ever been. It could be your childhood home, being with a grandparent, or even lying on a beach in Hawaii. Whatever that place is for you, concentrate on it for the next few minutes. Visualize what it was like to be there. How did you feel in that safe and serene environment? Let the feelings wash over you until you can feel your muscles relax. Now, doesn't that feel better?

The fact is, there are many things over which we do have control. We decide what we eat, how we deal with stress, and whether we exercise. The benefits outweigh the costs in so many ways. Short-term benefits include less stress and a greater feeling of well-being. Long-term benefits include reduced risk of heart disease, diabetes, stroke, and the list goes on. The question is, are you focused on the short-term pain or the long-term gain? The choice is yours.

APPLICATION

This week, "promote" yourself to become the Senior Director of Your Mind and Body, and think of at least two changes you can implement for your health. When you get stressed, take a one-minute visual vacation break (think about the Bahamas, for example). Look for any excuses that get in the way of staying healthy. Are they real obstacles? Or only imagined? What can you do to clear away the barriers and focus on your health?

EVALUATION & JOURNAL

On Friday, think about the following questions as you prepare to journal.

1. What did you notice about your eating habits? What could be changed to give you a better, higher level of sustainable energy?

2. How well did you cope with stress? Were you able to give yourself a one-minute vacation?

3. Were you able to make exercise a priority, or did you find excuses? Why?

4. What weekly fitness goal could you set for yourself – that you could positively commit to meet? Does making such a commitment frighten or motivate you? Why?

_____

_____

_____

_____

_____

_____

_____

_____

_____

_____

_____

_____

_____

_____

_____

_____

_____

_____

_____

_____

When You're Wrong, Say So.

CONCEPT

Have you ever wondered why it so difficult to say, "I made a mistake" or "I'm sorry?" Somehow, we feel we have to defend ourselves, even when we're wrong. The problem with that strategy is that it sets us up for others to take potshots at us. So, admitting a wrong is a concept that cuts two ways.

If we don't admit our mistakes, we come across as arrogant and egotistical – the exact traits that make others want to criticize us. They know we've erred. *We* know we've erred. When we fail to come clean, people see us as being deceptive, and they distrust and resent us. A great saying that describes this well goes something like this: If we humble ourselves, others will lift us up. But if we elevate ourselves, others will try to tear us down. The quicker we can clear the air, the quicker the wounds can heal. So, don't be afraid to admit wrong and apologize. Others will respect us much more than if we constantly try to cover our tracks. The upside of admitting when we're wrong is:

- It's proactive … and it keeps others from pointing it out to us!
- It releases us from carrying it around so we can move on and concentrate on solutions.
- It helps us focus on achieving results instead of placing blame or defending our ego.
- It clears the air and creates peace; it disarms potentially explosive situations.

Now, think about how you feel toward someone who has wronged you but refuses to apologize? You start to distrust and resent them, don't you? The problem is, if we allow these feelings of resentment to take root inside of us, they eventually yield terrible consequences. We become bitter and unforgiving. Author Malachy McCourt said it best: "Resentment is like taking poison and waiting for the other person to die." For our own personal well-being, we cannot afford to develop and hold grudges against others.

We can't let petty grudges go to seed inside our minds. Even when these grudges seem well justified, they only hurt us in the end. Think about it. When we resent someone, they are, in many ways, closer to us than a friend. We spend more time thinking about that person than we do those we love. That's not healthy. So, give it up. Move on.

APPLICATION

This week, focus on two things: admitting when you are wrong and forgiving others when they wrong you. Look for opportunities to admit, apologize, and clear the air – no matter how small the incident. Think about how you feel before and afterward. Next, make a list of any unresolved injustices that you are carrying around in your head. Those incidents that upset you but never got resolved. Once you've made your list, counter each injustice with the statement, "This probably wasn't about me. This was their own issue." Or, you may want to try, "So what?" or "Who cares?" Now, forgive them. Notice and record when you start to feel the "freedom" of dumping this old load of resentments.

EVALUATE & JOURNAL

On Friday, think about the following questions as you prepare to journal.

1. Journal for two minutes about the phrase, "There is no one closer than someone you can't forgive." What does it mean, and how does it affect YOU?

2. Describe how easy or difficult it was for you to put your ego aside and admit your errors. Why? What did you learn about yourself? How will this revelation help you in the future?

3. Did you find you were holding on to old grudges? Describe how you rationalized them in your mind. How did you finally release them and let them go? How did this make you feel?

4. Do you know anyone to whom admitting wrongdoing and forgiving others comes easily? How has it benefited them in their career? If they seem to be more well adjusted in life, what can you learn from their success in this area?

_____

_____

_____

_____

_____

_____

_____

_____

_____

_____

_____

_____

_____

_____

_____

_____

_____

_____

_____

_____

_____

_____

Develop Your Empathy for Others.

CONCEPT

It is so easy to jump to conclusions about others, isn't it? A man was driving very fast down the freeway, swerving in and out of cars, barely avoiding an accident. Drivers all around were visibly upset, honking at the driver and making obscene gestures. Then, he suddenly exited the freeway where a huge sign read "HOSPITAL." I can only imagine what agony he must have been in, possibly racing to the hospital where a loved one was sick or dying. Of course, we'll never know the reason. But it doesn't matter. What is important is that we try to put ourselves in the other person's place and imagine what life must be like from their perspective.

Our workplace offers us many great opportunities to practice empathy. Take the single mother who comes in a few minutes late looking very tired. We could take a hard line over those three minutes and judge her harshly. Or we could imagine how it would feel to leave our sick child at home – or with a stranger. When you can feel what the other person is going through, you have empathy. Until then, you will most likely sit in judgment, find them guilty of violating some rule, and condemn them to a sentence of less tolerance, less pay, and/or less opportunity.

Am I saying that people should be allowed to come in late? Of course not. But there are times when it cannot be helped. It is during those instances that we can, and should, be empathetic toward the other person. They probably need our help and understanding much more than they need our judgment and criticism.

APPLICATION

This week, look for opportunities to develop your empathy. For example, find someone who is new to the job, and imagine what it must be like to be new and not know what to do. Find a way to coach and help that person. Remember, you were a beginner once, too!

EVALUATE & JOURNAL

On Friday, think about the following questions as you prepare to journal.

1. How did you do in developing your empathy this week? Were you able to put yourself in the other person's shoes? How did it affect your judgment of that person?

2. Do you think a supervisor can have empathy for others and still be an effective manager? Why or why not?

3. Do you know anyone who is skilled in this area? How are they perceived by the people with whom they work? Why do you think employees are more loyal to supervisors they trust?

Focus on Results, Not Activities.

CONCEPT

Many times, I hear employees say, "Oh, I am so busy. No one works as hard as I do." I always think, "That may be true, but are you producing results?" Bosses don't want to pay for activities. Those activities have to produce results … and the quicker the better. True, some of us have jobs where results are difficult to quantify. However, we should always be focused on three areas of our business: maximizing productivity, increasing sales or revenue, and lowering costs. If we focus our efforts on these areas, our bosses will be happy.

Here's another example. Do you know anyone who overcommits? They say "yes" to everything and pretty soon they can't accomplish anything? I tend to do that a bit myself. But I've learned (the hard way) that it is always better to undercommit … and overdeliver. Missing even the smallest deadline by two hours can leave people questioning your ethics and abilities. But beating a deadline by an hour or two can make a lasting positive impression. How do you want to be remembered?

So ask yourself: Am I busy working hard? Or am I busy producing results? Focus on results, and you'll see your boss focusing more on you and your career development!

APPLICATION

This week, take a good look at how you spend your time. Are you just busy, or are you delivering the goods? Ask yourself, "What is it about my work that should impress my boss or my company?" If you can't think of anything, then you can assume your boss can't either. Now, start looking for ways that you can exceed expectations. Again, focus on results. Don't get bogged down in the details or the activities.

EVALUATE & JOURNAL

On Friday, think about the following questions as you prepare to journal.

1. In evaluating your past performance, did you find that you were more focused on busy activities or on productive results? If activities, why? How do you think it has affected your boss' perception of you?

2. What did you do that exceeded your boss' expectations? Did your boss notice? What kind of feedback did you receive?

3. Do you know anyone who is a fast, efficient, results-oriented worker? Make friends with that person. Find out what they do that makes them so efficient. How can you model what they do to improve your own skills?

Be Extraordinary in Everything You Do.

CONCEPT

A recent judicial candidate being interviewed by the legislature was asked who had been the biggest influence in her life. She replied, "My grandmother." She went on to say that her grandmother told her she must be extraordinary in everything she did. Even if it was just washing dishes for a living, she was to be the best, most extraordinary dishwasher ever.

What a great lesson for each of us. The being and the doing come straight from the heart. If we love what we do, it shows. Conversely, if we don't love what we do, that also shows. Oh, we can put in a pretty good day's work, even if we hate our jobs, but it will be the little extras that we miss. Why? Because we won't care enough to notice that level of detail. So, in the end we'll be ordinary … not extraordinary.

Remember, everything we do exemplifies who we are and what is important to us. Artist Norman Rockwell once said, "Every work is a self-portrait of the person who did it." So, how is your self-portrait looking? Are you proud of the work you do? Does it show? What does it say about you as a person?

"There's no traffic jam on the extra mile."

— Anonymous

APPLICATION

This week, take a critical look at the quality of your work. If it were someone else's product, how would you rate it? Poor, average, or way above average? Be honest. Remember, someone else (namely, your boss) is already looking at it that way! Next, select at least two areas of your work where you could make an improvement: in quantity or quality. Your goal this week is to produce something extraordinary! That could be something as simple as giving a customer extraordinary customer service – you know, the kind that is so memorable they tell all their friends about your company. Or it could be in the product you produce. Whatever it is, make it extraordinary!

EVALUATE & JOURNAL

On Friday, think about the following questions as you prepare to journal.

1. After taking a hard look at the quality of your work, how did you rate yourself? Was it difficult to look at your work objectively, like your boss does, and rate it? Did you find yourself becoming defensive? Why?

2. Which part of your work did you select to be extraordinary? What actions or steps did you take to move the quality or quantity up a few notches? Did it involve a change of heart or attitude adjustment? Explain.

3. Most importantly, how did you feel after turning in extraordinary work? Did you feel a boost to your self-esteem? (You should have.)

4. How can you keep this higher quality/quantity mindset going? What would it take for you to feel passionate enough about your job that you did everything with excellence? What do you think the long-term benefits might be?

Know What's Important.

CONCEPT

There's a saying, "don't sweat the small stuff." What that really means is that most small stuff is not important. Not really. And most successful employees know this. They have sufficient "tread on their tires" that allows them to face life's ups and downs with relative ease. They can absorb small issues that don't matter in the big scheme of things. They have the ability to stay focused. They know with laser-point precision which things matter – and which things don't – and they keep their attention focused on what is important.

Let's look at some examples. Successful employees:

- Develop a tolerance for the little indiscretions of others and overlook others' weaknesses.
- Know how to make their time count. They don't get caught up in rumors, gossip, or other unproductive behavior.
- Take calculated risks. They understand the ratio between risk and reward and can make sound decisions that support the company's goals.
- Know what is most important to the company and support it. For example, they support the safety program because they understand how high incidences of injuries can affect both productivity and costs.
- Know when to cut their losses. If something, or someone, is not working out, they know how important it is to cut their losses sooner rather than later.

In short, they focus on the big stuff – the stuff that affects the company's profitability and productivity.

APPLICATION

This week, look for opportunities to focus on what is important to your employer. Is it safety? Compliance? Costs? Productivity? Sales? Identify at least three areas where you can "overlook the small stuff." Identify at least one co-worker who constantly hooks your emotions. What can you do to give them a little more tolerance so you can focus on what's important to the business?

EVALUATE & JOURNAL

On Friday, think about the following questions as you prepare to journal.

1. What is important to your employer? Record it.

2. How well were you able to adjust to the big picture and overlook the little stuff this week? In what areas are you still feeling challenged?

3. How were you able to overlook your co-workers' little irritations? What can you do to improve this skill?

4. Do you know anyone who is very adept at staying focused on the big, important stuff? How do they do it? What can you learn from them? How has this skill helped them in their career success?

_____

_____

_____

_____

_____

_____

_____

_____

_____

_____

_____

_____

_____

_____

_____

_____

_____

_____

_____

_____

_____

_____

CONCEPT

I work with an amazing woman who can rattle off facts, numbers, and statistics at any time, without any preparation. I once asked her, "How do you know all that stuff?" She replied, "I make it my business to know what is going on." This lady is definitely on top of her game. And she has won the respect and confidence of everyone on our top management team.

Another woman with whom I work is a highly successful personnel recruiter. When I inquired about her tips for success, her story was similar. She said, "You have to constantly be on top of your game! You have to know your candidates, remember their names, know their strengths and weaknesses … and then know the same things about your customers. If you don't, you'll miss opportunities to make the great matches." By being on top of her game, this woman enjoys the financial freedom that few other employees do.

So, how do we get "on top of our game?" By putting some skin in the game. "Putting skin in the game is a slang term that means you are willing to make a significant personal commitment to your career. So, what are the characteristics these high achievers have in common? First, they love what they do. To them, it's fun! Second, they take their job seriously. They think about it, plan for it, and work it all the time … even after hours. Third, they stay in shape. They get enough sleep, they take the time they need to recharge, and they maintain strong support systems.

I don't know if there is any magic formula, but one thing is for sure. If you want to be on top of your game and impress your boss, you must be willing to make the personal commitment – however that is defined in your line of work. It may mean reading up on company literature to educate yourself about your organization. Or it may mean taking a class to learn a new software program or a new method of cost-accounting. Whatever it is, if you put some skin in the game, you'll be respected for your efforts.

APPLICATION

This week, take a hard look at your own level of commitment to your career. Are you on top of your game? Do you make the required investment of time and energy to stay on top of things? If you don't, now is the time to start. Next, review the high-achiever characteristics above. Do you love what you do? Do you take your job seriously? Do you stay rested and keep your energy level high? Come up with your own formula for success. Pick at least two areas where you can make improvements, and make a list of what you will do specifically to improve your game.

EVALUATE & JOURNAL

On Friday, think about the following questions as you prepare to journal.

1. How did you rate yourself in terms of being "on top of your game?" Are you an A-player or ripe for a trade?

2. What specific steps will you take to become an A-player? What will it take to impress your boss? Or to come to the attention of top management? Are you willing to make that level of commitment? Why or why not?

CONCEPT

How many of us are afraid of failure? If honest, we would all raise our hand. But the real question is HOW afraid are we of failure? Are we so afraid that we won't try anything? Or are we just slightly afraid but willing to try something new? Where we are on that continuum is a function of our self-confidence. If we associate failure with fear of criticism or rejection, we'll throw in the towel. But if we associate failure with the opportunity to learn and grow, we'll get up and try again.

Let's take a hard look at failure and see if we can figure out why it causes us to fear. First of all, failure simply means to err or miss, to be unsuccessful in some endeavor. Well, we've all been there. In fact, some of our greatest heroes have been failures at some things. Who do you think this is?

> *When he was 22, he failed in business. When he was 23, he ran for the legislature and lost. When he was 24, he failed in business again. . . . When he was 29, he was defeated for the post of Speaker of the House in the State Legislature. . . . When he was 34, he ran for Congress and lost. At the age of 37, he ran for Congress and finally won. Two years later, he ran again and lost his seat in Congress. At the age of 46, he ran for the U.S. Senate and lost. The following year he ran for Vice President and lost that, too. He ran for the Senate again, and again lost. Finally, at the age of 51, he was elected President of the United States. Who was this perpetual "loser"? Abraham Lincoln.* [5]

The point is, it is impossible to avoid failure altogether. So, instead of letting failure totally incapacitate us, let's look for ways to use failure in our favor. Remember, failure does have a positive side. First, it keeps us humble. It makes us fertile ground for seeds of learning. Second, it is a great teacher. Inventor Buckminster Fuller once wrote, "Whatever humans have learned had to be learned as a consequence only of trial and error experience. Humans have learned only through mistakes." [6] Failures show us what doesn't work so we can try again to see what does work.

Finally, the adversity that failure brings actually makes us stronger. For example, W. Mitchell overcame two life-threatening and life-changing accidents to become an author (*It's Not What Happens To You, It's What You Do About It,*) TV host, and sought after motivational speaker. [7] Lance Armstrong overcame cancer to become a world-champion cyclist. And of course there is Bill Porter, who overcame cerebral palsy to become Watkins' top-grossing salesman in the United States. The list goes on. But you get the point – adversity makes us stronger.

APPLICATION

This week, answer the question, "What would you like to accomplish *if* you knew you could not fail?" Write that on a sheet of paper. Now make two columns under your dream, and write "Pros" on the left side and "Cons" on the right side. Under "Pros," write down all the advantages you could enjoy by overcoming your fears and pursuing your dream. Under "Cons," record all the disadvantages of pursuing your dream. Remember what author Earl Nightingale said: The time is going to pass anyway. Why not have something to show for it?

EVALUATE & JOURNAL

On Friday, think about the following questions as you prepare to journal.

1. Inventor Thomas Edison once said, "Many of life's failures are men who did not realize how close they were to success when they gave up." Think about that, and journal for two minutes.

2. How could Edison's quote apply in your own life? Think about your own fear of failure. What is driving it?

3. As you thought about what you would like to accomplish if you knew you couldn't fail, how did it make you feel? As you recorded all the pros and cons of pursuing your dream, what did you find out about the source of your fears? Are they real or imagined?

4. What will you do to overcome your fears and pursue your goals? What kinds of possibilities could this lead to over time? How could it help you enjoy greater career success?

_____

_____

_____

_____

_____

_____

_____

_____

_____

_____

_____

_____

_____

_____

_____

_____

_____

_____

_____

_____

_____

_____

Set Your Own Standards of Excellence.

CONCEPT

Many employees wait for the boss to tell them what to do. Sometimes, they even say things like, "That's not in my job description," or "I wasn't asked to do that part of it." Then, if they haven't been told what to do, they stand around and wait for the next order or direction.

How do you think management perceives this attitude? Right. That person is perceived as someone without initiative, who cannot make things happen without direction. That isn't the impression we want to make if we want to be a vital part of the team.

Successful employees do just the opposite. They find out what the company's standards of excellence are. Then, they set about to exceed those standards. They don't wait for someone to tell them ... or show them. They just do it.

Want to be successful in your job? Then:

- Do more than you are expected to do.
- Give more than you are expected to give.
- Listen more than you are expected to listen.
- Work harder than you are expected to work.

Don't take my word for it. Try it for a week. See if it doesn't make a difference! Corporations are looking for "can do" people who will take initiative. And most of them are willing to pay for it!

APPLICATION

This week, look at your own level of performance. Do you take the initiative ... or wait to be told what to do? Are you perceived as being proactive or reactive? Your goal is to take steps to improve your performance and change any negative perceptions. You can still impress the boss – but get busy, starting today!

EVALUATE & JOURNAL

On Friday, think about the following questions as you prepare to journal.

1. How would you rate your level of "excellence" on a scale of 1 to 10, with 10 being extraordinary?

2. What would you have to do to make your rating a 10? What change would you need to make?

3. Are you willing to do that? Why or why not?

_____

_____

_____

_____

_____

_____

_____

_____

_____

_____

_____

_____

_____

_____

_____

_____

_____

_____

_____

_____

_____

_____

Motivate Yourself (And Others).

CONCEPT

Management books tell us that motivation is either internal (intrinsic) or external (extrinsic). So to motivate ourselves, we must understand what spurs us to action. If we are externally motivated, we will do things as a means to an end – say, for the promise of a reward, promotion, money, praise, or approval. If we are internally motivated, however, we will do things simply for the enjoyment of the activity itself [8], or for how it makes us feel. Feelings of accomplishment, connectedness to others, contribution, success, confidence, or autonomy are all possible internal motivators.

The point is, we must know ourselves and keep ourselves motivated. Some people may think, "Well, that's my boss' job." Not so. Not every boss has the skill or ability (or time) to recognize what motivates others. So, it is up to you. Set up your own reward system. Need an idea? How about, "When I complete the exercises in this book, I will reward myself by ..." and select something that has value to you. Or "When I complete my next semester in school, I will reward myself by ..." Don't wait for someone to read your mind. Make it happen on your own.

Now, what about motivating others? How can we apply this lesson? First, make it one of your goals to develop the skills needed to "understand others." Next, work on your confidence in asking the kinds of questions that identify other people's motivations. (For example, "What is more important to you – your working environment or relationships? Why?") Then, use your influence to set up situations where others not only get their needs met, but also feel motivated in the process. Remember – it must be about them and for them. Never, ever use fear as a motivator. And never use motivation as a manipulator to get what you want. Motivation is others-centered, but manipulation is self-centered. Finally, be sure to acknowledge the achievement when someone reaches a goal. Remember, it must be sincere.

APPLICATION

This week, take a close look at the kinds of things motivate you. Why do you do what you do? What keeps you going? What makes you feel fulfilled and challenged? Those are the things that motivate you. Next, design two or three questions that will help you find out what motivates others. Spend some time with an employee (or co-worker) and find out what challenges and satisfies them. Finally, look for an opportunity to guide their job or task in an area that will make them want to exceed every expectation.

EVALUATE & JOURNAL

On Friday, think about the following questions as you prepare to journal.

1. After making your list, did you find that you are more internally or externally motivated? Was this a surprise? Why?

2. Now that you know what motivates you, how can you design your work around those motivators? What would it take? Are you willing to pay the price?

3. Who did you select to interview and identify their motivators? What did you find out? Is that person internally or externally motivated?

4. Were you able to redesign an activity or task to generate personal satisfaction for them? How did it make you feel about yourself and your role in the other person's life?

Be a Lifetime Learner.

CONCEPT

Changing technology is continually affecting our work environment and how we do our jobs. For many of us, that means we need to constantly update and expand our skills. Which skills? Well, not only our technical skills. Most people could benefit immensely from improved interpersonal skills too.

In fact, organizations are on the lookout for people who can effectively express themselves and manage their emotions. Have you ever noticed that it is the people with well-honed people skills that seem to rise to the top? That's no mistake. The whole idea behind management is to get things done through other people. And the best way to get things done through others is by effectively communicating the organization's goals – and then inspiring others to *want* to follow your leadership.

So, in pursuing continual learning, let's focus on:

- Becoming a lifetime learner. Never stop feeding and challenging your mind.
- Being willing to learn. Just because you've been around a long time doesn't mean you know it all. We can learn a lot from each other.
- Watching the "input" to our minds – what we read, watch, hear. For example, reading a skill-improvement book or listening to a motivational tape will improve our skills more than watching TV. Remember: garbage in, garbage out.
- Reading motivating words of wisdom. Like this book!
- Bringing added value to your job. Be a continual learner … even if you're not in school.

APPLICATION

This week, read, listen, and learn for at least an hour every day. You could read an educational book or listen to a motivational tape. Pick one or two items from the list above and look for opportunities to learn something new. Rather than saying, "That's not my job," ask, "What can I learn from this situation?" Be on a continual quest for knowledge.

EVALUATE & JOURNAL

On Friday, think about the following questions as you prepare to journal.

1. What did you discover about your learning habits? In what areas could you be doing better?

2. Do you know anyone who is an avid reader or who is taking classes? How has their quest for knowledge affected their job? What kinds of opportunities have opened up to them?

3. What can you learn from this? What will you do, starting now, to become a lifetime learner?

_____

_____

_____

_____

_____

_____

_____

_____

_____

_____

_____

_____

_____

_____

_____

_____

_____

_____

_____

_____

_____

_____

part
2

WORKING WITH THEM:

INTERPERSONAL SKILLS FOR SUCCESS

Build Successful Relationships.

CONCEPT

Building relationships. Now, why would this be an important skill to have in business? Because everything we do, every goal we have, and every result we achieve is based on successful relationships.

Let's think of relationship-building as a process ... not a one-time event. Relationships are based on trust and are built and nurtured over time. It takes time to establish what Stephen Covey calls "an emotional bank account." [9] This is the litmus test of trust in the relationship. In other words, when the account balance is high, we can make a withdrawal (favor, mistake, error, etc.) without it having a negative impact on the relationship. But if the account is low, any kind of withdrawal could bankrupt the relationship.

How do we build these relationships? By building and cultivating trust. We do what we say we are going to do. By networking, both inside and outside the organization. By remembering the little things, such as people's birthdays and other special events. By personal touches, such as sending flowers or a card. All of these show that you consider the other person important and that you care about them. All of these interactions make deposits and build successful relationships over time.

APPLICATION

This week, pick one or two relationships that you would like to take to the next level. List three or four things that you will either say or do to make that person feel important. Make some deposits in the person's emotional bank account. Even if you are uncomfortable, send at least one hand-written note. It may sound old-fashioned, but it works. I know when I get one, it is always memorable.

EVALUATE & JOURNAL

On Friday, think about the following questions as you prepare to journal.

1. How did you do at building relationships? Did it feel awkward, or did it come easily? Why do you think that is?

2. How did you identify which relationship to "take to the next level?" What specifically did you do or say to make deposits in that person's emotional bank account?

3. Reflecting back on the week, how successful was this exercise? How do you think this could help you in your professional career, especially if you continued to practice it over time?

4. Do you know anyone who is good at building relationships? How has it helped them achieve success in their career? What can you learn from them?

Learn to Deal with Difficult People.

CONCEPT

As a little girl in Minnesota, I rode the school bus every day. One of my bus drivers, Myron, used to sing "My Bonnie Lies over the Ocean" [10] every morning as I got on the bus. I hated it. I thought he was trying to humiliate me, and I was embarrassed. I told my mother I was never getting on that school bus again. Well, she used this situation as an opportunity to help me build my interpersonal skills. While I don't remember her exact words, the "message" was this: There will always be "Myrons" in your life. They'll look different or have a different name, but if you don't learn to deal with this Myron, then you'll never learn to deal with other kinds of people either.

And isn't that true? People we consider difficult come in all shapes, sizes, ages, and genders. And until we learn to get along with them, they will continue to show up in our lives – with different names and different faces. Many people act contrary simply because they want attention. Or because they feel underappreciated.

So, what's the best way to deal with the people we find difficult? Ask yourself what their underlying needs are – what is making them act the way they do? Then, come up with a way to help them meet that need. Remember, saying "thank you" costs nothing – yet it produces a huge return. Saying thanks and making someone smile is a gift that is free and easy to give. It is one of the most important interpersonal skills we can learn.

Myron, I realized, sang to me on the bus because he liked me and wanted to make me feel special. And once I realized that, I learned to smile and thank him. In fact, since I was the last stop for the school bus each day, we would often sing little tunes together as we rode along. Now, years later, I still think of Myron every time I hear, "My Bonnie Lies Over the Ocean."

APPLICATION

This week, identify the "Myron" in your life. What is it about that person that bothers you? Next, think of something you could do or say that would make that person feel special – that might meet some unmet need. Make it a point to smile and greet everyone you meet at work. And say "thank you" to at least two people every day! Then, watch how people respond to you.

EVALUATE & JOURNAL

On Friday, think about the following questions as you prepare to journal.

1. Who turned out to be your most challenging person? What unmet needs do you think they have? What did you do to help meet that need?

2. Did you work on your smile? Think. How many times did your smile get returned?

3. What did you learn from this experience? What value from this lesson can you apply in the future? What kind of impact could having great interpersonal skills have on your career in the long run?

_____

_____

_____

_____

_____

_____

_____

_____

_____

_____

_____

_____

_____

_____

_____

_____

_____

_____

_____

_____

_____

Learn to Ask Intelligent, Probing, Clarifying Questions.

CONCEPT

So many misunderstandings happen because we fail to ask questions. We tend to take things at face value instead of asking "why," "when," "how," or "what if" questions. I'm reminded of an incident where a co-worker reported a half-story to the CEO. Instead of asking questions to clarify (and thereby uncovering the truth), the co-worker passed the story on in its half-baked form. Naturally, the CEO became upset when he realized he'd wasted time and energy on a benign situation. If the story had been checked out first with clarifying questions, his energies could have been spent on more important things.

Is this happening in your company? Are meritless "stories" getting passed around, and are corporate energies being wasted on nonproductive activities? Think about it. Where could your company be today if everyone were asking "how" and "what if" questions first? These are great questions because they cut through the fluff and get us focused on results. In other words, it gets us past placing blame and on to solving problems.

So, asking intelligent, probing, and clarifying questions is not only good for business, but it also helps develop better relationships. I like what poet and philosopher Henry David Thoreau once said: "The greatest compliment that was ever paid me was when one asked me what I thought, and attended to my answer." Imagine how you would feel if your co-worker or boss asked you for your thoughts and opinions. You would feel honored, I'm sure. Well, that's something each of us could, and should, do for others. Asking questions demonstrates that we have an open mind. It also shows that we are neutral, out of the politics, and open to new ideas and perspectives.

APPLICATION

This week, focus on keeping an open mind. Ask intelligent, probing questions. Question any rumor or story and refuse to take it at face value. Ask "why" or "how" questions (as in, "Why does this person find it necessary to criticize others?"). Then ask "what if" questions (as in, "What if it isn't true?" or "What if that isn't what he or she meant?"). Remember, there are always two sides to every story. Next, make it a point to ask others for their input, opinions, and ideas. Watch and notice how people change towards you.

EVALUATE & JOURNAL

On Friday, think about the following questions as you prepare to journal.

1. Describe any opportunities you had to question a rumor or story. What was it like for you to ask probing questions? Did you feel empowered by inquiring about "the rest of the story?"

2. How did people respond to you when you asked questions? Were they able to answer your "why" or "how" questions, or did they only have surface information? How did it make you feel about the reliability of that person's story?

3. When you asked others for their input, opinions, and ideas, describe the types of reactions you got from others. Was it a positive or negative experience? Why?

4. Identify at least one person who is skilled at asking probing questions. Describe how you perceive that person. How do you think their ability to ask questions has affected their career success?

Watch Your Words – And Your Tone.

CONCEPT

One day, my husband, David, asked our five-year old grandson Justin if he wanted to go out for some French fries. When Justin asked why, David replied, "Because we're buddies." Justin said, "I already have a buddy. His name is Jason, and he is really cool," to which David replied, "Well, Grandpa's cool too." Justin looked down, thought a minute, then softly said, "Grandpa, you are really special … but you are not cool." Harsh words? Maybe. But they were spoken honestly, and with love, straight from a child's heart.

The truth is, what you say is not as important as how you say it. That's why tone of voice is so important. We can say almost anything to anybody, if we say it in a heartfelt and sincere tone. So, when tone is coupled with nonverbals (such as body stance, arms, head position, expression of eyes and mouth), it sends a powerful message.

That said, what you say can be powerful too. Words can be used to sooth or agitate emotions – to edify and lift up … or hurt and tear down. We don't think of words, in and of themselves, as having power. But if we think of words as living entities – that, once spoken, can never be taken back – we see just how much power they actually have. My grandmother had a great metaphor for this. She said that to say something unkind or unfair about someone is like taking a big feather pillow outside on a windy day, cutting it open, and shaking it as hard as you can until all the feathers have blown away. Then, once we realize that we've spoken too harshly or unfairly, our task is to go back and gather up all those feathers that blew away in the wind. Quite an impossible task. So it is with the words we speak. It is always better not to speak them in the first place.

Here are some additional skills for being an expert communicator:

- Use your words to build people up. Never use your words to destroy another person.
- Never say anything about anyone that you would not want repeated in a court of law. Why? Because that's where our words of discrimination and/or harassment could eventually end up.
- Always begin conversations by asking, rather than telling.
- Always use "I" language when addressing unwanted or inappropriate behavior. Never start a criticism with the word "you."
- When you ask others to do something, always phrase it in the form of a request. Never demand. Being demanding is one of the shortest paths to career disaster.

APPLICATION

This week, watch your words very carefully. Think about everything you say before you say it! Watch your tone of voice. Are your words benign but your tone abrasive? Intentionally look for opportunities to use your words to compliment others. Stop criticizing … if only for the week. Refuse to speak badly of anyone. Reflect on the metaphor of the feathers in the wind. Anticipate the lasting damage your words could have. Finally, actively seek opportunities to speak well of your company, your boss, and your co-workers.

EVALUATE & JOURNAL

On Friday, think about the following questions as you prepare to journal.

1. What did you learn this week about your tone of voice? Did you find that your tone is sometimes harsher than you thought? How did you find out?

2. What about your words? How difficult was it for you to spend an entire week without saying anything negative, complaining, or criticizing others? Why do you think that is?

3. Were you able to compliment and praise others? What positive things did you specifically say about your company, your boss, and your co-workers? Did it change how you felt about them?

Listen More Than You Speak.

CONCEPT

When my husband was a stockbroker, there was a plaque on the wall that read: "In a single day, Samson slew a thousand Philistines with the jawbone of an ass. Every day, thousands of sales are killed with the same weapon." In other words, sales are lost when people don't listen.

Great point. In fact, have you ever considered that most people don't really care what you think or have to say? And that most people would rather talk than listen? I used to work with a guy who would frequently say, "Let me ask you a question." But there was never a question mark at the end of his next statement. In fact, his statement had no end. What he really meant was, "I want to talk. But I'm going to let you think that I want your opinion." These one-sided conversations could go on for several minutes, but there was never a question forthcoming. He had simply wanted to talk.

So, what can we learn from this? If most people have an unquenchable desire to be heard and rarely, if ever, want to hear what you have to say, the ability to listen becomes critical. Stephen Covey, in his 7 *Habits of Highly Effective People,* [11] calls it "listening with empathy" – in other words, listening from the heart. Empathic listening means we are listening for content as well as emotions. As people struggle to find the right words to express their pain, they frequently cannot tell us where they hurt. They may even use words that could get us off-track (the content). But if we are tuned in to their emotions, we'll understand what they are trying to say.

Another reason why listening is so important is because when we are talking, we are not learning. Listening is an important skill in building better relationships. Being listened to makes us feel understood, valued, and worthwhile. It also clarifies expectations and eliminates misunderstandings.

> *"We have two ears and one mouth so that we can listen twice as much as we speak."*
> — *Epictetus, second-century Greek philosopher*

APPLICATION

This week, look for opportunities to listen, listen, listen. First, consider the above quote from Epictetus. Next, learn to ask open-ended questions and then listen for content and emotion. What is the person trying to say? Encourage the person to keep talking by paraphrasing their words and saying such things as, "I see" and "Tell me more." Finally, listen with your heart. Try to see life from the other person's viewpoint. What are the underlying emotions the person is trying to express? Do the person's words and emotions match each other? If not, why not?

EVALUATE & JOURNAL

On Friday, think about the following questions as you prepare to journal.

1. Journal for two minutes on the saying "A wise man listens more than he speaks." Why do you think wisdom is associated with listening?

2. As you asked questions and then listened, how often was there an inconsistency between the person's words and their emotions? Why do you think that happened?

3. How did being an active listener increase your empathy for others? How do you think this skill can help you in your career?

_____

_____

_____

_____

_____

_____

_____

_____

_____

_____

_____

_____

_____

_____

_____

_____

_____

_____

_____

_____

_____

Give More Than You Take.

CONCEPT

Did your parents or grandparents live through the Great Depression? If they did, it undoubtedly changed them forever. My family certainly had vivid memories of those days. As a little girl, I remember getting tired of hearing the same old stories over and over again. One day, my dad said, "I hope you never experience a depression, honey. But if you do, remember one thing: always give more than you take."

Obviously, not everyone had Depression-era parents. For example, I once had an employee tell me, "If you will pay me more money, I'll do a better job." After recovering from the shock, I replied, "If you do a better job, I may pay you more money." I was briefly confused but then realized that everyone is socialized differently.

The point is, we live in a country where there is an abundance of everything. It would be easy to take advantage of the system and take more than you give, if you were so inclined. What's the upside? Well, you might just get by with it … for awhile. What's the downside? It ruins your character. It fosters an "entitlement" mentality. It eventually causes you to feel dishonest, deceitful, and fraudulent. Giving more than you take is not about what it does for others – your family, your boss, your employer. It's about what it does for you.

Here are some ideas of ways to give more than you take:
- Work an extra hour without getting paid for it. Do more than is expected.
- Always do your best. Nothing less. Ever.
- Do something for someone who can never repay you.
- Be willing to make a sacrifice in the short term; you'll see rewards in the long term.
- Never, ever say, "That's not my job."
- Do something that really knocks your boss' socks off – something that demonstrates your tangible or intangible value to the company.

What happens if you start to give more than they take? You win the support and admiration of your co-workers and boss. In fact, your boss may want to give you a raise before you even ask for it!

APPLICATION

This week, read the list of ideas above. Select one or two to complete this week. Look for ways give, to go an extra mile. This exercise is not about getting – but giving. Notice how it makes you feel about yourself.

EVALUATE & JOURNAL

On Friday, think about the following questions as you prepare to journal.

1. Reflect on the quote, "Give an honest day's work for an honest day's pay." What does that mean to you?

2. Which of the above ideas did you select to do this week? Record your experiences. Did anyone notice your good work? Did you receive an acknowledgment or thanks? (Don't worry if you didn't. This exercise was about how it made you feel.)

3. How did you feel when you gave more than you took? Was there a positive sense of accomplishment, or are you waiting for the payback? Why do you think that is? How do you think an attitude of giving could enhance your career success?

Be Others-Centered, Not Self-Centered.

CONCEPT

Tami was blessed with a huge capacity to care about others. And it was genuine – it just came from her heart. During the time we worked together, I was always amazed by her ability to focus on the needs of others. She remembered people's birthdays. She always had a word of encouragement. And most important, I never heard her bad-mouth the company or her co-workers. But more than that, she took the initiative in building relationships. She was always the first to ask, "How are you doing? Are things going well? What's new in your life?" It was never about her.

What a contrast with most of the people with whom we work! I'm sure you can think of several colleagues who are completely self-absorbed. In fact, most of us have no problem being self-centered. And some of us actually believe that the universe revolves around us and our needs. If that is our mindset, it'll take a huge effort to get our eyes and thoughts off of ourselves and focused on others.

A couple of years later when Tami left our company to return to school, our CEO told her how much we would all miss her and her "5000-watt attitude!" What a compliment. Being others-centered certainly had value in the eyes of our CEO.

APPLICATION

This week, look for opportunities to edify others. Here are some additional ways you can be others-centered:

- Make someone feel important by showing genuine interest in them and in what they have to say. Ask questions. Seek opinions.
- Do something nice for someone, without expecting anything in return.
- Make sure what you say behind someone's back could be said to their face.
- Pray for others. It'll help you be less concerned about yourself.
- If someone shows anger, say something kind in return. Help to de-escalate their anger. Be part of the solution.

EVALUATE & JOURNAL

On Friday, think about the following questions as you prepare to journal.

1. How difficult was it for you to focus on others rather than yourself? What did you learn from that insight?

2. What specifically did you do that made someone else feel important? Did you remember to ask questions? How often did you seek someone else's opinion? What were the results?

3. How did this particular activity help you become more aware of others' feelings and needs? How do you think this new skill could help you in your career path?

Be Humble.

CONCEPT

On a recent flight from Denver to Los Angeles, a young man sat down in the seat next to me. Before the plane left the terminal, he had engaged me in conversation. He asked questions and appeared to be very others-centered. This was of great interest to me since most people like to talk about themselves. When I began to ask him about himself, he revealed that he was trying to become a better person. Interesting comment. When I asked him to explain, he stopped for a moment, looked down, deep in thought. Then, he admitted that he has not had much success in finding a good job and was really struggling to find his career path. He said he realized that he had been imitating his parent's attitudes about life: defensive, arrogant, take what you can get. Obviously, it had not served him well. He was now trying a new approach: humility. Being interested in others. In fact, he was on his way to an interview in Los Angeles. I gave him my card and asked him to call me so I could set up an interview for him with our company!

What does it mean to be humble? The dictionary calls it being modest or meek in behavior or attitude. This may not sound very appealing in our "me first" society. But this is what it looks like in the workplace:

- Be kind to those of less stature (or power).
- Be respectful of everyone … regardless of their station in life.
- Forget about your own ego. Remember, it is not about you.
- Offer assistance. Do tasks you think are beneath you.
- Be open to correction or criticism. Look for insights into your own blindside.
- Ask others for their help. Or ask for their opinion.
- Never, ever abuse your power. It is a shortcut to sudden career death.

Do you want to know what happened to the guy on the plane? He did call me. He landed a great job (before we even had a chance to interview him!). He was happy and excited about his new opportunity. Know what? I think it was because of his brand-new attitude. We can all learn a lesson from this. Humility will serve us better than any other attitude I can think of. Lack of humility will produce opposite results.

APPLICATION

This week, look for opportunities to show interest in others … especially those you feel are below you in rank. For an entire week, refuse to talk about yourself. Only ask others about themselves. Ask questions. Solicit opinions. Be curious. Notice whether people are more open with you. Look for opportunities to build mutual trust. Then, offer to do something for someone to make their job (or their life) a little bit easier. I think you will be amazed at the difference an attitude of humility will make in your life.

EVALUATE & JOURNAL

On Friday, think about the following questions as you prepare to journal.

1. What did you learn about your level of humility?

2. Where you would rank yourself on a continuum with arrogance on one end and humility on the other? If you rate higher on the arrogance side, what can you do to get over yourself?

3. If you know anyone who demonstrates humility in the workplace, ask him or her for coaching in this area. How helpful has humility been in their career? How could this help you?

Stay Upbeat. Emotions Are Contagious.

CONCEPT

Ever come in to work on a Monday morning, feeling just a little bit down? And then you run into that positive, upbeat person who is always having a good day? I had the good fortune to work with a guy like that one time. I don't think Sam ever had a down day ... or if he did, we never knew about it. He just had the incredible ability to see the positive in every situation and in every person. When he'd see you in the hallway, he'd say something like, "Good morning. Beautiful day, isn't it?" Or "Great rain we had last night, wasn't it?" He always had a big smile. You couldn't help but feel better just by being around him.

While it wasn't a conscious decision, I made Sam one of my role models. I decided to start each day by getting up on the "right side of the bed." I decided to give a friendly greeting to people whenever possible and to try to make their day just a little bit better because they had interacted with me. Did I always succeed? Of course not. But over time, I found it easier and easier to actually believe it was a great day ... regardless of the circumstances. I hope I can bring a moment of happiness to everyone with whom I interact – whether at the coffee machine at work or in the checkout line at the grocery store. I believe that, over time, caring about others can help change attitudes, emotions, and self-esteem.

"Yeah, but how do I stay upbeat in down times?" you may ask. Good question. It's not easy. It is in the down times where the rubber meets the road. Anyone can put on a happy face when life is good. It takes an extraordinary person to find the positive thread in a company layoff or lost account. But can you see the value of such a person? Companies are desperate for employees who will choose the high road, keep their emotions in check, and help others transition smoothly. Talk about adding value! You, and your attitude, could be the catalyst that makes all the difference between success and failure.

APPLICATION

This week, make it a point to get up on the right side of the bed. Every day. Greet everyone you meet with a friendly good morning and a genuine smile. Even if you have to fake it, do it. Then, make a conscious effort to influence the emotions of those around you. If others are negative and complaining, help them identify something positive. If they're feeling down, do something special that will perk them up. If they're feeling lonely, offer to take them to coffee. If they're feeling unappreciated, find something about their work for which you can genuinely compliment them. No, you don't have to be the boss to compliment others. A genuine and heartfelt compliment is welcome anytime.

EVALUATE & JOURNAL

On Friday, think about the following questions as you prepare to journal.

1. Describe how easy or difficult it was for you to consciously "get up on the right side of the bed." Did you struggle with putting on a positive attitude, or did it come easily to you?

2. What kind of difference did it make in your own emotions as you started your day? Did things look a little brighter to you as well?

3. How were you able to influence the attitudes and emotions of others? Could you see their emotions brighten just a little after having interacted with you?

4. How will you keep this practice going? What do you think it will do for you in the long run?

_____

_____

_____

_____

_____

_____

_____

_____

_____

_____

_____

_____

_____

_____

_____

_____

_____

_____

_____

_____

_____

_____

_____

Develop a "Service Mentality."

CONCEPT

How many of you can remember President John F. Kennedy saying, "Ask not what your country can do for you but what you can do for your country?" What if we changed that phrase slightly by substituting the word "organization" for "country?" What kind of impact do you think a change in attitude could have on the success of our organizations? Immediately? Over time?

Bob was like that. He was a senior-level executive, but he had the heart of a servant. He frequently worked incredible hours to help his team meet contract deadlines. He was willing to roll up his sleeves and do the same work he expected of others. In fact, in a crunch, he would outlast us all. It is no wonder he had the admiration and respect of everyone – superiors and subordinates alike.

This concept of service is just as important in the world of sales. Max Sachs International is a sales training organization. One of the first principles it teaches is that salespeople only earn the right to call on prospects "when they can be of service." [12] What a novel thought. You mean, it isn't about the salesperson "getting a sale?" Nope. It's about the salesperson "giving a service." One of the participants in a sales training class once said, "Oh, I finally get it. Sales isn't about me getting. It is about me giving." Right on.

APPLICATION

This week, look for opportunities to serve others – maybe your co-workers or your boss. Offer to do something extra and totally unexpected. Perhaps offer to work an extra hour every day this week without getting paid for it. Do more than is expected. If your boss wants you to do something by 5 p.m., do what you have to do to get it done by 3 p.m. Exceed expectations. Remember, it is not about what you can "get," but what you can "give." Remember, even Jesus was willing to get down on his hands and knees and wash the feet of the men who worked for him.

EVALUATE & JOURNAL

On Friday, think about the following questions as you prepare to journal.

1. Journal for two minutes on the statement "Ask not what your organization can do for you but what you can do for your organization." In what ways could you do more for your company? How could it benefit you?

2. What was your biggest struggle this week as you looked for opportunities to serve others? How did it feel? Foreign or comfortable?

3. Where did you decide to focus your attention? How did others react to you? Did anyone express appreciation?

4. Most important, how did you feel about yourself? Did this give you a sense of satisfaction? How do you think this attitude of giving could impact your career, and your life, in the long run?

_____

_____

_____

_____

_____

_____

_____

_____

_____

_____

_____

_____

_____

_____

_____

_____

_____

_____

_____

_____

_____

_____

_____

CONCEPT

Power is an interesting concept. We generally think of power in negative terms – as in, "That person has a lot of power" or "That person's power has sure gone to his head." When people abuse their power, it certainly has negative consequences. It reminds me of something an acquaintance of mine once said: "Power is something you have until you use it [inappropriately]. If you ever use it, you lose it."

But let's think of how power can be used in a positive way. Our CEO once said, "If you want to have more power, give away the power you have." In other words, by sharing our power, or empowering others, we inadvertently strengthen our own power base. The simple act of sharing power says, "I trust you. I believe in you. I have confidence that you can do the job." Imagine how people will feel about you when you extend the olive branch of trust.

The by-products of empowering others are many, including:

• Strengthening and growing your employees.

• Giving others opportunities to be successful.

• Creating a mutual purpose among co-workers.

• Building trust. Remember, trust builds respect. And mutual respect builds strong organizations.

• Keeping yourself humble. Nothing corrupts more than absolute power. So share what you have.

APPLICATION

This week, look for opportunities to share your power with others. You have no power, you say? Oh, yes, you do. At the very least, you have the power to influence others and their opinions (about themselves, about your company, about your boss). If you are a supervisor, then use your power to build the skills of others. Find ways to create opportunities for others. Then, watch what happens to people's attitude about you.

EVALUATE & JOURNAL

On Friday, think about the following questions as you prepare to journal.

1. Write your thoughts about the statement: "Power is something you have until you use it. If you use it inappropriately, you lose it." What do you think that means? Come up with at least one example of someone who abused their power. How did their abuse of power affect their success in the long run?

2. What other positive by-products of empowering others did you discover? How did it make you feel about yourself?

3. How do you think an attitude of sharing power could affect your career over time? Is there any down side to sharing power? In the short term or the long term?

4. What did you learn from this experience? How will it change how you supervise/work with others in the future?

Tell The Truth. Be Honest.

CONCEPT

Early in my career, I placed an ad in the *Los Angeles Times* and transposed a couple of digits in the phone number. When I realized it, it was too late – the ad was already running. It would have been easy to blame the advertising department … or even the newspaper. But I knew the error was mine. Unfortunately, the error was costly, and I was afraid of the consequences. However, when I finally mustered the courage to tell our CEO what I had done, he calmly said, "Well, what do you think we can do to fix the problem today?"

Telling the truth might not be easy, but it is always the right thing to do. Yes, the consequences could have been bad. But lying about it and blaming others would not have fixed the problem – which was the ultimate goal! And I would have alienated the other people on my team. Why is this important? Because it demonstrates our level of integrity. Oh, I've made plenty of mistakes since then. But I've found that telling the truth is always the best solution.

Here are some other ways to always tell the truth:

- Walk your talk. Do what you say you are going to do.
- Acknowledge when you don't know something. There is no shame in saying, "I don't know, but I'll find out and get back to you."
- Don't ever steal from your company. If you feel you are due something, talk to your boss about it. Stealing is a shortcut to early career death.
- Give more than you get. The scales will eventually weigh in your favor.
- Be sincere in everything you say and do. Insincerity feels like manipulation and causes distrust.
- Speak honestly about others. Refuse to gossip or tell stories that may not be true.
- Always do the right thing. It may not be popular, or comfortable, but eventually your company, your boss, and your co-workers will respect your integrity.

APPLICATION

This week, follow through on everything you said you would do. Work overtime if you need to, just to meet your deadline. Look for opportunities to say something good and positive about another person. Refuse to engage in gossip or storytelling. Notice how people began to respond differently to you. Do you sense an increase in trust or respect? If so, your integrity is beginning to show through.

EVALUATE & JOURNAL

On Friday, think about the following questions as you prepare to journal.

1. What did you learn about your level of honesty and integrity? Where is there room for improvement?

2. If you were to only speak the truth, how do you think it would affect your career success? What are the pros of telling the truth? The cons?

3. How do you feel about people who always speak openly and honestly? Do you have more, or less, trust for them? What can you learn from this exercise?

_____

_____

_____

_____

_____

_____

_____

_____

_____

_____

_____

_____

_____

_____

_____

_____

_____

_____

_____

_____

_____

Change Perceptions: Yours and Others'.

CONCEPT

Everything matters. "Like what," you may ask. Like everything. Like the way we speak. The way we act. The way we express ourselves. The language we use (good and bad). Our physical appearance. Even whether or not our nails are clean and our shoes are polished! It all counts toward creating the important first impression. There is an old saying: "You only get one chance to make a good first impression." How true it is! If others perceive us negatively (whether they're right or wrong), it is an uphill battle to change that perception.

Many years ago, a young man in our computer department showed up for work one day sporting a brand-new eyebrow piercing. Mind you, this was back in the day when that was quite shocking. I learned an important lesson through that experience. People's attitudes about him changed … for the worse. Oh, sure, he was still the same guy. Same intelligence. Same education. Nothing changed except his eyebrow ring. But he was perceived as not being a team player because he no longer fit in with the corporate culture. All of a sudden, it became much more difficult for him to demonstrate his worth. Unfair, you say? Perhaps. On the other hand, we can't dictate how others perceive us. Right or wrong, it is what it is. Once that attitude is formed, however, it can take years to regain what was lost.

Perceptions are simply insights – a certain way of seeing or understanding something. Unfortunately, initial perceptions often happen in a heartbeat. Changing those perceptions can take a lifetime.

Want to improve others' perceptions of you? Here are some other insights that can help:

- Adopt a service mentality. Look for opportunities to do something totally unexpected for someone else. Note their reaction.
- Be willing to do the little things – you just never know when it might lead to something bigger – like opportunities!

APPLICATION

This week, think about perceptions you hold of other people. On what criteria are they based? Something the person said or did? Is it a fair perception, or has it been biased by your own values and opinions? Begin to look for opportunities to change your perceptions of others. Look for something good in everyone. Try to understand why they do what they do … or say what they say. What internal needs do they have that are not getting met? Now, do something totally unexpected for that person. Go the extra mile for them, and see how it affects them. Better yet, see how it affects their perception of you.

EVALUATE & JOURNAL

On Friday, think about the following questions as you prepare to journal.

1. What did you discover about your perceptions of others? Were they fair or biased?

2. Was there an opportunity for you to change someone's opinion or perception of you? What did you say or do that worked? Can you do more of that in the future?

3. What did you learn about yourself? Did you discover any old attitude that has created a barrier to your success? Did you discover that people may have been perceiving you incorrectly? If so, what have you done in the past that gave them that impression? If it is true that "everything matters," what can you do in the future to upgrade your reputation?

_____

_____

_____

_____

_____

_____

_____

_____

_____

_____

_____

_____

_____

_____

_____

_____

_____

_____

_____

_____

_____

_____

Be Supportive of Your Boss.

CONCEPT

No, I'm not recommending that you play politics. But I am recommending that you think of, and treat, your boss like your number one customer. Why? Because she or he is! If you fail to serve this customer well, you may find yourself in the unemployment line. But that's not the only reason you should support your boss.

Let's look at some ways to make this concept feel more natural and less contrived. Suppose you are a supervisor (or if you already are, pretend you are a senior-level executive). You were probably promoted into your job because you were a strong individual contributor. You knew the technical part of your job really well or you produced more than anyone else. Or perhaps you had some type of special skills. Whatever the reason, you were the one selected for promotion.

Think back to that day. You probably went to work on a Friday as a team contributor, got promoted, and started Monday morning as a supervisor! Sure, you were excited about the opportunity. However, you probably didn't get any training along with the new job. You were just expected to know what to do and get the job done. You may have continued doing what you had always done, and it may have even appeared like nothing much had changed. Inside, you had your doubts. You wondered if you were doing the right thing. You wondered if anyone knew that you didn't really know what you were doing. Scary, right? Well, unfortunately, that is the life of many supervisors.

Now suppose you have a certain employee who is your "go to" person. They assist you and are willing to do whatever it takes to help you get the job done. They give you solid, well-thought-out feedback. They make sure your department meets its production goals. They stand up for you and support you. They make you look good to upper management. They genuinely do everything they can to give you the kind of support you need to do the best job you can. Tell me, what would that person be worth to you? How much would you be willing to pay someone for that kind of loyalty and support? My guess is: the sky is the limit.

Become that kind of employee (or supervisor). Someone who is unquestionably supportive of the organization and who is known as someone who will not compromise the trust their employer has placed in them. You'll probably find great rewards for your efforts – perhaps a raise or a promotion of your own!

APPLICATION

This week, look for opportunities to support your boss and your organization in what you say and do. Even if you personally disagree with a policy or practice, support it. Assume there is a good reason for it. Present a united front. Refuse to blame or accuse. Watch out for self-limiting attitudes and refuse to say statements like, "It's not in my job description." Next, look for ways to partner with your boss and build a better relationship. Remember, you don't have to be best friends with your boss, but you do have to be respectful and supportive. When your boss is successful, then you will be successful too.

EVALUATE & JOURNAL

On Friday, think about the following questions as you prepare to journal.

1. How difficult was it for you to see your boss or organization as trustworthy? What obstacles did you have to overcome to find small ways to build trust?

2. Journal about any opportunities you found to make your boss look good. What did you say or do that furthered their cause? Did you receive acknowledgment for it?

3. What do you see as the biggest obstacle you'll have to overcome to live the rest of your corporate life this way?

4. Do you know anyone to whom this kind of support and loyalty comes naturally? How has it affected their career success over the long run? How do you think it could affect yours?

_____

_____

_____

_____

_____

_____

_____

_____

_____

_____

_____

_____

_____

_____

_____

_____

_____

_____

_____

_____

Don't Try to Be a Buddy to the Boss or Vice-Versa.

CONCEPT

Pat and Jim had worked together for years. When Jim became a supervisor, neither of them could see any reason to change the relationship. One Friday evening while the team gathered for happy hour, several people began to discuss the most recent rumor of a potential company relocation. Emotions began to simmer. Many people voiced fears about losing their jobs.

After the group ordered another round of beers, Pat turned to Jim and announced, "Well, we just happen to have someone from management here. Jim, why don't you tell us what is really going on over at the plant?" Jim squirmed and said he didn't know anything. Pat continued to press for answers, stating that several of the workers had recently bought cars or homes and had debts to pay. Pat said, "We need to know the status of our jobs, and you owe it to us to tell us what is going on." Jim was in an uncomfortable situation, and he finally found an excuse to leave. But on Monday morning, he faced the grueling job of reprimanding a former co-worker.

The truth is, that invisible line between you and the boss should never be crossed – by either of you. On occasion, bosses (or employees) may be inclined to disclose personal information and gossip about themselves. In my experience, both parties usually come to regret it. Situations change. Relationships change. We've all heard the phrase by author Mark Twain, "familiarity breeds contempt." Don't put yourself in a situation where you invite or know too much about your boss. Or vice versa.

APPLICATION

This week, look for opportunities to "hold the line." Don't solicit or tell inappropriate information. If and when you feel tempted to tell more about yourself than you should, stop. Think of others who like to gossip about themselves. Is the gossip welcome? How do people end up feeling about that person? And finally, do you think it serves any good purpose in the workplace?

EVALUATE & JOURNAL

On Friday, think about the following questions as you prepare to journal.

1. What did you notice? Was it difficult to keep your personal distance from your boss? Was it difficult to not gossip about yourself?

2. Think about others who do gossip about themselves. How has it affected their relationships (or reputation) over time? What is the lesson to be learned here? How can you use that lesson to your advantage? How can you use to increase your effectiveness in your job?

3. Now, journal what you have learned. Share any insights you have gained.

_____

_____

_____

_____

_____

_____

_____

_____

_____

_____

_____

_____

_____

_____

_____

_____

_____

_____

_____

CONCEPT

In earlier lessons, we've focused on asking questions and admitting wrongdoing. Why? Because it's a shortcut to conflict resolution. Think about it. If we err – and admit it – we can move on. Case closed. Or if we ask questions and get clarification on the issue, then we can focus on solutions. Again, case closed.

But if we aren't able to resolve our own conflicts, they will eventually escalate to the place where our employer becomes involved. I've seen this happen over and over again in Human Resources. Something small and incidental happens. Neither party addresses it. Soon, it comes to the supervisor's attention. But the supervisor either can't or won't address it. Then, it escalates to the place where "sides" begin to form around the two parties, and other staff gets involved. What started out as a simple little wound now begins to fester and eventually infects the entire workplace. When it reaches the place of all-out aggression, the company has to step in and try to resolve it.

Imagine the amount of wasted time, energy, and resources. Now, think of what could have been accomplished if everyone had been focused on resolving the problem quickly and moving on.

So, let's compare the value of two employees: One employee takes personal responsibility for his/her own actions and resolves problems quickly. The other employee refuses to take responsibility for the issue or resolve the problem. One is part of the solution; the other is part of the problem. Which one do you think has more value to the organization? If you were the owner of your company, would you want your employees focused on positive, business-building ideas … or acting out their aggression over small, insignificant issues? The answer is obvious. Corporations are looking for employees who take responsibility for resolving their own issues and then get back to the task at hand.

APPLICATION

This week, look for opportunities to resolve your own issues … quickly. Think of it as a game. If you can resolve your issue in less than 24 hours, you win! If the issue goes on longer than a day, or if HR has to get involved, you lose. Literally and figuratively.

Next, develop a scorecard for your department. Make two columns: "Profit" and "Costs." Now, based on the activities of you and your co-workers, begin to keep score of all your activities, conversations, and other work-related issues. Are the activities of your team adding to the profit side of your company or the cost side? Now, project these results out over the next year. What kind of impact will you, and your co-workers, have on the company's bottom line? Finally, a tough question. If you were your boss, would you be seen as adding value or draining profit from your organization?

EVALUATE & JOURNAL

On Friday, think about the following questions as you prepare to journal.

1. As you addressed personal issues this week, did you have a winning score or a losing score? Why do you think that happened?

2. Now, how did your team score? Is the team adding value or draining profits from the company? What could be the long-term result if things continue as they are?

3. Identify at least one person who is good at addressing and resolving issues before they become a big deal. How do you and others feel about that person? Are they seen as solution-oriented?

4. How has that person's ability to resolve issues quickly affected their career success? What can you learn from them?

_____

_____

_____

_____

_____

_____

_____

_____

_____

_____

_____

_____

_____

_____

_____

_____

_____

_____

_____

_____

_____

Assume the Other Person's "Good Intentions."

CONCEPT

What we extend to others, we usually get back. More specifically, how we view other people's intentions is usually a direct reflection of our own motives. In other words, if we have dishonest or unscrupulous motives when dealing with others, we'll no doubt assume that they have dishonest or unscrupulous motives toward us as well. But if we believe that most people have positive motives and good intentions toward us, we will almost always give them the benefit of the doubt. Remember, you must believe in your own goodness before you can see it in others.

Why is this such an important concept? Because of how it affects us and our behaviors. Not the other person, but us. Assuming the worst in others makes us cautious, suspicious, and surly. Assuming the best in others, however, makes us courteous, trusting, and approachable. Which mindset serves us best? Which mindset helps us achieve our goals? Which mindset builds cooperative relationships in the workplace? Assuming best intentions leads to positive career results.

Here are some additional benefits of assuming good intentions:

- When we assume best intentions, we can overlook people's little indiscretions.
- It keeps us objective. Instead of "telling stories," we can ask questions and look for valid reasons for behavior.
- We become more tolerant. We're more balanced so we can absorb things without letting them upset us.
- We can change the attitudes of others by extending understanding and tolerance.

APPLICATION

This week, make it a point to assume others' good intentions … at least until you get the whole story. Ask clarifying questions and seek input before you judge the other person's motives or intentions. In his book *Nonviolent Communication*, [13] author Marshall Rosenberg says that "anything that anyone does is an attempt to fulfill unmet needs." This week, try to understand what "unmet needs" others may have. Then, give them the benefit of the doubt and look for ways to help satisfy those needs.

EVALUATE & JOURNAL

On Friday, think about the following questions as you prepare to journal.

1. Journal for two minutes about Rosenberg's quote, "Anything a person does is an attempt to fulfill unmet needs." What do you think this means? How could this change your initial attitude about a person who has offended you?

2. How difficult was it for you to avoid coming to a conclusion until you had all the facts? Were you able to use your "questioning skills" to find out more information? How did finding all the facts affect your conclusions?

3. How have you let speculation and suspicion color your opinions in the past? How has "assuming best intentions" given you the space and freedom to draw your own conclusions?

4. Identify someone who has this skill and uses it well. Ask them to mentor you when you have issues and seek their big-picture perspective. How has this skill helped them enjoy a successful career?

_____

_____

_____

_____

_____

_____

_____

_____

_____

_____

_____

_____

_____

_____

_____

_____

_____

_____

_____

_____

_____

_____

_____

Recognize and Compliment Others.

CONCEPT

Have you ever worked with someone who is a stellar performer – who works hard and puts out tons of work? Who is loyal and has a great attitude? Now, may I ask … how many times have you complimented that person yourself? Probably not very often.

Most of us wait for the boss to notice a top performer. It is the boss' responsibility to compliment or reward that person, right? Not necessarily. Who says we can't recognize and compliment each other? True, we may not have the same level of authority. But wouldn't you rather have a compliment from a co-worker than none at all?

I believe it takes a confident person with a gracious spirit to see and recognize great performance in others. Most of us are too self-centered to notice other people's accomplishments. But think of the affect this attitude of "giving recognition and compliments" could have on an organization. Isn't this the kind of company where you would want to work?

> *People may not remember exactly what you did, or what you said, but they will always remember how you made them feel.*
>
> *– Unknown*

APPLICATION

This week, look for co-workers or subordinates who do a great job. Take the time to tell them so. Be specific. You don't have to get the words just right, as long as the other person understands that you appreciate and recognize their hard work. Now, find at least one boss or superior that you can compliment. Make sure it is sincere. Remember, bosses don't get a lot of compliments. Why can't one come from you?

EVALUATE & JOURNAL

On Friday, think about the following questions as you prepare to journal.

1. Reread the quote above, then journal about it for two minutes. Why do you think it is true?

2. Who were you able to recognize and compliment this week? What type of reaction did you get from the person? Did you at least get a smile or a thank you?

3. More importantly, how did it make YOU feel when you complimented someone else? Didn't your step feel just a little lighter too?

4. Do you know of anyone who is skilled in this area? (If not, find someone.) Journal for a couple of minutes about how this skill has helped that person enjoy career success. Why do you think that is so?

Be Kind – Make A Difference in Someone's Life.

CONCEPT

A candidate came in to a recruiting office for an interview in a sleeveless blouse and a crumpled skirt – hardly appropriate attire for an interview with an upscale client. Assuming the candidate was dressed as well as she could afford, the manager ran to a store and bought a jacket to match the skirt. The new jacket fit and gave just the right impression. She went for the interview, wowed them, and got the job. And she got to keep the jacket. In my book, that's an act of kindness that made a huge difference in that candidate's life.

Here's another story: The CEO of a company I once worked for only visited our location once or twice a year, but when he did, he always asked that Mark pick him up at the airport. Mark was our maintenance guy, an elderly man who was still working so he and his wife could raise their grandchildren. Our CEO made a point of making this employee feel special, even though he had a lower status position. Just imagine if you were Mark. Wouldn't you feel special? What would that single act do for your attitude and loyalty toward the company? And it did just that too. It's no surprise that Mark was the most loyal employee we ever had.

We must show respect and kindness to everyone – regardless of their station in life. In our country of plenty, it is easy to feel insignificant and without value. Each of us, however, has the power to change those feelings in others – just by acknowledging them and being kind.

APPLICATION

This week, perform at least one act of kindness each day. You don't have to spend any money on this project. Simply acknowledge someone who is usually overlooked or thank someone who usually gets no thanks. Greet someone in the hallway who is usually ignored. Remember the CEO I mentioned? He rose to the top of a Fortune 500 company, primarily because of his great interpersonal skills.

EVALUATE & JOURNAL

On Friday, think about the following questions as you prepare to journal.

1. How difficult was it for you to find someone in need of special attention?

2. How did it make you feel to acknowledge and recognize that person? Did you at least get a smile in return?

3. How did this exercise change how you feel about yourself? Did it give you a feeling of satisfaction?

4. Did you find yourself being more thankful for what you have after focusing on people who have less than you?

5. How could having this skill help you reach your career goals?

Find a Mentor. Model Their Behavior.

CONCEPT

If you ask successful people what helped them reach success, most will tell you they had a mentor. Someone who gave them wise advice and guidance and helped them move ahead in their career.

Over the years, I've been fortunate to have mentors at several different stages. However, one stands out above the rest. Bill was an engineer by education but was quite well read in the areas of psychology, management, and human behaviors. We were working on forecasting at the time, and he coached me through setting up Excel spreadsheets to run regression analyses. We identified dependent and response variables and plugged them in to predict future sales of a division. This exercise exhausted me. It was like drinking water from a high-pressure water hose. But I learned more about Excel in those few weeks than I would have in a year of school.

His management style was also impressive. Was he tough? Oh, you bet. But fair. He always held people accountable. He always listened … and gave advice only if you asked for it. In fact, I don't think he ever "gave" me advice but instead used a Socratic method [14] of asking questions that helped me discover my own answers. He was a great mentor for me. In the two years I worked for him, I learned so much, so fast, that I used to say, "Learning under him is like baptism by blowtorch." But I did learn … and enjoyed it. And I have used him as a role model in many ways.

APPLICATION

This week, look for and identify a mentor. It can be someone with whom you work or someone outside the workplace. If you can't think of anyone, call the local Rotary or other business organization and ask if they know of anyone who could mentor you. One of the things you will learn from any good mentor is, "Don't be afraid to roll up your sleeves and work hard." Use your mentor to strategize and plan your moves at work. Find out what they've done to be successful. Then, try to be like them. Make it your life's goal to be someone's "best boss ever." Wouldn't that be a worthwhile accomplishment?

EVALUATE & JOURNAL

On Friday, think about the following questions as you prepare to journal.

1. Who will be your mentor? Why did you select that person?

2. What is it about their management style that you like? Why do you want to be more like them?

3. If you met with your mentor, what questions did they ask to get you thinking?

4. How has their style helped them be successful in their career? What can you learn from that?

Be Careful about the Company You Keep.

CONCEPT

We've all heard the phrase "You are judged by the company you keep." This is true in business as well as our private lives. I once worked with a very capable, smart, results-oriented performer. Unfortunately, she developed a reputation for hanging out with the party animals in the company. Soon, her image and credibility were in the tank, and she was no longer considered for higher-level management opportunities. Unfair, you say? Maybe. But from the organization's perspective, it made good economic sense.

There's another way of looking at our associations with others. Consider what Jim Rohn (American businessman, author, speaker, philosopher) once said:

> *You must constantly ask yourself these questions: Who am I around? What are they doing to me? What have they got me reading? What have they got me saying? Where do they have me going? What do they have me thinking? And most important, what do they have me becoming? Then ask yourself the big question: Is that okay? Your life does not get better by chance, it gets better by change.*

Perhaps Robert Levine, author of *The Power of Persuasion*, [15] said it best: "Good reputations are difficult to acquire but easy to lose. Bad reputations are easy to acquire and difficult to lose."

APPLICATION

This week, take a good look at the company you are keeping. Be open and objective. Ask yourself the same questions as noted in the Jim Rohn quote above. Are your friends helping you move closer to, or further away from, career success?

EVALUATE & JOURNAL

On Friday, think about the following questions as you prepare to journal.

1. Reread the above quote by Jim Rohn. Reflect on what it says, and journal about it for two minutes.

2. As you consider the company you are keeping, are these friends helping or hurting you? Do you like who you are becoming when you are with them?

3. If the answer above is "no," what can you do to begin easing off these relationships and nurturing new ones? What kind of commitment will you make to achieve this goal? What kind of timeline will you give yourself?

_____

_____

_____

_____

_____

_____

_____

_____

_____

_____

_____

_____

_____

_____

_____

_____

_____

_____

_____

_____

_____

Stay Out of the Politics.

CONCEPT

Anyone can get involved in corporate politics. But it takes a self-confident achiever to stay above the fray. Unfortunately, many people get sucked into the mudslinging, to no good end. I'm sure we have all seen a few good people bite the dust because they found themselves on the wrong side of the political arena.

Let's consider politics from a organizational standpoint. The goal of an organization is to get the job done (products manufactured, items shipped, services provided, etc.). We need people to help us reach that goal. Specifically, we need people with a cooperative attitude and a strong work ethic to help us reach that goal. It's not just about getting the product out the door. It's about getting it out the door faster, better, and cheaper than the competition. That's how we're evaluated in the marketplace.

It sort of reminds me of being in school. In school, we not only have to do the homework, but we also have to get along with the other kids. We get graded on how well we do both scholastically and socially. In other words, that's how we're evaluated in the academic system.

The same thing is true in organizations. Most companies cannot afford to tolerate political players, especially if they have a divide-and-conquer agenda. So, where is the safest place to be? Right in the middle, totally focused on getting the job done. If we always make it our goal to do our job and get along with people, we have nothing to fear from the politics going on around us. Playing politics is a lose-lose proposition.

APPLICATION

This week, survey the politics where you work. Whom has formed what type of alliances? How does it work? Why does it work? Ask yourself, is the company better or worse off because of the politics? How could getting rid of the politics have a positive impact on your organization? Be prepared to give specific examples when you journal.

EVALUATE & JOURNAL

On Friday, think about the following questions as you prepare to journal.

1. How did you find out about the politics and the political players at your place of work? Is it under control, or are politics running rampant? Why do you think that is?

2. Do you know anyone who is very adapt at staying off the radar screen and building positive alliances with everyone, regardless of where they are politically? What is it that they do well? What makes them successful?

3. What is the downside of playing politics at your particular organization? What can you do to personally influence others to "stay above the fray?" How do you think this type of influence could benefit you both personally and professionally?

_____

_____

_____

_____

_____

_____

_____

_____

_____

_____

_____

_____

_____

_____

_____

_____

_____

_____

_____

_____

_____

_____

_____

CONCEPT

My husband and I recently rented the movie *The Merchant of Venice,* based on the play by William Shakespeare. The most memorable scene, in my opinion, was the one of Shylock, the Jewish moneylender, pleading with his anti-Semetic counterparts to consider him as a fellow human being. In a wrenching and heartfelt plea for equity, Shylock says:

> *Hath not a Jew eyes? Hath not a Jew hands, organs, dimensions, senses, affections, passions; fed with the same food, hurt with the same weapons, subject to the same diseases, heal'd by the same means, warm'd and cool'd by the same winter and summer. . . . If you prick us, do we not bleed? If you tickle us, do we not laugh? If you poison us, shall we not die?* [16]

It reminds me of something my mother always told me, "Never, ever make fun of another person for their appearance, their nationality, the color of their hair, the way their face is shaped, or anything else." Why? Because we don't get to choose those things about ourselves. We don't get to choose which family we are born into … or our nationality … or the language spoken in our home. No one is any better or any worse than another, and we must never forget that words said in fun still hurt. In fact, I know many adults today who can still remember with vivid clarity hurtful things that were said to them when they were children. And for some, it happened several decades ago! Yet those words still hurt as if they were said yesterday.

In the workplace, there is never any excuse for bad behavior. And there is certainly no excuse for making fun of others because of their age, race, sex, national origin … and all of those other categories legally protected under Title VII of the Civil Rights Act. Oh, we know it is against the law. But I still hear it on occasion. I'll bet you do too. It's just like we learned in an earlier lesson, words can be used to lift up or tear down. Make it your goal to stick up for and defend those who cannot defend themselves.

APPLICATION

This week, be on the lookout for people who might need a friend. Pay particular attention to anyone who is the brunt of any jokes or inappropriate language. Come to their defense. Make a point of lending your support and helping them cope with an embarrassing situation.

EVALUATE & JOURNAL

On Friday, think about the following questions as you prepare to journal.

1. Read and journal for two minutes about the following quote from author Robert Fulghum: "Sticks and stones may break my bones, but words can break my heart."

2. Have you ever personally experienced a hurtful taunt? How did it make you feel? What did you do about it? Were you able to defend yourself? How did it affect your self-esteem going forward?

3. Did you find anyone this week that needed an assist? What was the situation? How easy or difficult was it for you to intercede on the other person's behalf? Why?

4. How do you feel about people who readily step in and defend others? Do you wish you could be more like them? How does it affect your level of respect for them? Why?

Be Curious. Look for Options.

CONCEPT

How many times have you heard the statement "We've always done it this way." In other words, if it worked in the past, why change it? Well, people used to think the Earth was the center of the universe too. But Copernicus and Galileo proved them wrong.

"Who cares?" you might ask. Well, we all should because we can learn from history. It is important that we not accept things just because "they've always been that way." Organizations that are bound up in this type of thinking find it difficult to stay competitive. Technology is changing all around us. It would be ignorant to think that there are no better ways to do things than "how we've always done them."

So, let's move past that mindset. Let's be curious. Let's ask "what if" questions, and look for options. Brainstorm better, faster, more efficient ways to get things done. Our CEO recently came up with a more efficient way of processing a national payroll. No, we had never done it that way before. But it has turned out to be more cost-effective with less errors. You can't beat that!

So, think about your company. Where are you stuck in a rut? What are some of the processes or procedures that are still being done the same old way? Think of how you could influence others to brainstorm and come up with creative new options. Coming up with options works well in employee relations as well. Dictating to someone how things are going to be is a lose-lose proposition. But brainstorming options and coming up with a solution that is acceptable to both parties is win-win.

APPLICATION

This week, look for opportunities to ask questions and create options. Find one process or procedure that you think could be done better or quicker. Now, think about how the same end result could be accomplished in less time or with fewer resources? Brainstorm your ideas with someone who also understands your processes. Be sure to have a solid idea for increased efficiency before you go to your boss. He or she will not want another project to evaluate … but they will be open to an idea that has been well-thought-out. Remember to present more than one option!

EVALUATE & JOURNAL

On Friday, think about the following questions as you prepare to journal.

1. Were you able to come up with any processes that are outdated? What were they? (Pick one or two about which to journal.)

2. Were your co-workers open to brainstorming new ideas? Why or why not?

3. Describe how you were able to make the process more efficient. Did you remember to present more than one option? How did your boss respond to your idea for increased efficiency?

_____

_____

_____

_____

_____

_____

_____

_____

_____

_____

_____

_____

_____

_____

_____

_____

_____

_____

_____

_____

_____

Develop a Reputation for Being a Problem Solver.

CONCEPT

One of my former bosses used to say, "Anyone can be a problem spotter. But if you bring me a well-thought solution, then you will be a problem solver."

Unfortunately, most people aren't born with this talent. In one of my previous jobs at a brokerage firm, I had a co-worker that was great at spotting problems anywhere and everywhere. One day, her computer would not turn on. It seemed like the 10th problem she had found that week, so in desperation we finally told her to call the repairperson. When the repairman showed up, he found that her computer accidentally had been unplugged by the maintenance crew. Simple solution. Just plug it back in.

I've thought of this incident many times since then because I think it is a lesson we've all had to learn. In fact, it makes me realize the incredible value of people who just naturally seek potential solutions whenever they discover a problem. Problem solvers are a special kind of people. They are:

- Proactive; they take the initiative to find solutions.
- Quick to anticipate the needs of others. They think about what might be missing and address the problem before it ever happens.
- Open. They ask questions because they realize opportunities come in lots of different packages.
- Brave. They're not afraid to jump in and try something new.
- Observant. They sense that everything around them is a lesson waiting to be learned.

Finally, problem solvers never stop to look for the equity or fairness in situations. They are all about the business of finding opportunities that are out there masquerading as problems.

APPLICATION

This week, actively look for problems in your workplace. They should be fairly easy to spot. Now, try to come up with creative solutions. Take the initiative to bring the problem – and the solution – to the boss' attention. Don't worry about getting credit … that will come later. Just focus on spotting, and solving, problems for your company. I'm confident that you'll be pleased with the results!

EVALUATE & JOURNAL

On Friday, think about the following questions as you prepare to journal.

1. Think of a time when you brought a problem to a boss but did not bring a solution. Knowing what you know now, how would you have handled the situation differently? What kind of difference could it have made in your boss' perception of you?

2. What did you learn about yourself during this exercise? Was it difficult or easy for you to recommend solutions? Did you feel comfortable or awkward making recommendations? Why?

3. Do you know anyone who is skilled in this area? What do they do that sets them apart from everyone else? Meet with that person and ask for some pointers.

Be the First to Give Credit and the Last to Take It.

CONCEPT

I once heard the phrase, "Give more credit; accept more blame." In our lesson on empowering others, we said that if you want more power, you must give away what you have. The same could be said of credit. If you want more credit, give away what you have. In fact, give credit to others even when it is only slightly due. Great managers look for opportunities to acknowledge and celebrate even small victories, because they know that little victories add up to huge successes over time.

By the same token, most organizations spend way too much time trying to assign blame. Does placing blame solve the problem? No. Does placing blame move us closer to a solution? No. Then what is the point? Poor managers will look for scapegoats among their people. But good managers will step up, accept more than their share of the blame, so the process can move on to the problem-solving stage.

See, it's never about you. Or me. It's about us, as a team. It's about all of us achieving a goal together. Management expert Ken Blanchard once said: "None of us is as smart as all of us." Meaning, none of us can accomplish much alone. But together, we can do great things. That's why great leaders also know when and where to fight their battles. They can overlook the little things, as long as the big goal is getting accomplished. They're quick to accept the blame when things get off-track. They're more concerned about achieving the goal than who or what it takes to get there.

President Harry S. Truman said it best when he said, "It is amazing what you can accomplish if you do not care who gets the credit." Isn't that true! Think about all the work-arounds and end runs that people do, just so they can get credit. Now think about how much more productive and profitable your company could be if no one cared who got the credit!

APPLICATION

This week, make it a point to share credit whenever you can. Look for opportunities to brag about someone else's contribution. If you receive credit, always make a point of sharing it with your team. And if things go wrong, offer to take the blame. I know that sounds difficult, but here's the magic of it. If you are at fault, then you are doing the right thing by fessing up. But if you are not totally to blame, others will know that too and admire you for "being big enough" to accept more than your share of the responsibility. Trust me, these are the things of great leaders. Remember Harry Truman's famous statement "The Buck Stops Here"? Let the buck stop with you.

EVALUATE & JOURNAL

On Friday, think about the following questions as you prepare to journal.

1. Reflect for a moment on the quote "It is amazing what you can accomplish if you do not care who gets the credit." If that were applied at your workplace, how would it affect your company's profitability? If you applied it in your own life, how would it affect your productivity? Journal for two minutes.

2. How did it feel to share credit with others? Did you get a feeling of empowerment? Why or why not?

3. How did it feel to take more than your share of the blame? Were you able to see that it brought issues to a close faster?

4. Identify at least one other person who models these skills. Watch how that person makes decisions, conducts themselves, and interacts with others. What can you learn? How have these skills helped that person be successful in his or her career?

Create a Positive Working Environment.

CONCEPT

Think of the best environment in which you have ever worked. What was it like? What were the people like? Were you more impressed with the décor or the interactions between co-workers?

The question is, how were *you* able to influence the environment? We tend to think that creating a pleasant working environment is up to the company. We think it is their responsibility to make sure there is an atmosphere of trust, support, and cooperation. Not so. Oh sure, they have some influence. But I believe the major contributors to a positive working environment are the employees themselves. You. Me. All of us. Regardless of our level or status in the organization, we can all have an impact on the working environment. Either positive or negative.

Here are some things you can do to help create a positive work environment:

• Be friendly. Smile.

• Have fun. Look for ways to make others enjoy what they do.

• Celebrate whenever possible. Birthdays, anniversaries, meeting a deadline, Groundhog Day, whatever. Just have a quick get-together.

• Keep the energy high. Create a sense of urgency. Make it fun.

• Build trust by holding each other accountable. Do what you say you'll do.

• Keep your door open – literally. Make it easy for people to interact with you.

• Cooperate with others. Offer to help someone else with a project.

• At the end of every day, say, "Thank you for your contribution today."

APPLICATION

This week, visualize the ideal workplace. Ask yourself, "What can I personally do to create more fun and energy in my work environment?" Record some of your ideas. Pick two or three areas you can influence and get started. At the end of every day, ask yourself how many times you made people feel better just by having interacted with you. Your goal is to be a positive influence … however small. Over time, it will create permanent change.

EVALUATE & JOURNAL

On Friday, think about the following questions as you prepare to journal.

1. How did you visualize the ideal workplace? Jot down some of the characteristics. Was it similar to one in which you currently work? Why or why not?

2. Which two or three things did you try this week? What kind of affect did it have? Did you at least cause a small ripple in the water? Don't give up! Change takes time, but eventually your positive attitude will have a lasting effect.

3. How can you keep these changes going? What obstacles do you anticipate? How can you work around those obstacles to achieve your goal? Identify someone who can be your advocate and partner for change.

_____

_____

_____

_____

_____

_____

_____

_____

_____

_____

_____

_____

_____

_____

_____

_____

_____

_____

_____

_____

_____

_____

Be an Expert at Improving Systems and Processes.

CONCEPT

Our world is changing faster than any previous time in history. We are no longer competing with the company down the street or in the next state. We are now competing globally, against countries with larger labor markets and fewer regulatory restrictions. How can we maintain our market share? How can we continue to thrive … and survive? We have to find ways to do what we do more efficiently. In other words, we need to be on the constant lookout for better, faster, more efficient ways of doing things.

Employees who are focused on making their organization more competitive are the employees who rise to the top. They intuitively know that organizations need three things to stay in business: increased productivity, increased profitability, and decreased costs … or some combination of these three.

Successful employees, then, take a critical look at their organization's processes. They look below the surface and beyond the obvious. They scrutinize each process for deviations that may be slowing down production or increasing operating costs. They ask "what if" questions to see if they can spot a more effective way to accomplish the same end result but in less time and at less cost.

Higher-level employees may also take a critical look at the organization's systems. For example, how could communication between interdependent departments of the organization be improved? They ask, "If a 1% improvement could be made, what could that save the company in a month, quarter, or year?"

MIT professor Peter Senge said in his book *The Fifth Discipline,* "We understand that the only competitive advantage the company of the future will have is its managers' ability to learn faster than its competitors." [17] It is the people with a "continual improvement" mindset that will be looking for ways to improve systems and processes and thereby improve faster than their competitors. Be a part of that process.

APPLICATION

This week, look for ways to increase your own productivity. We already know that successful people are more productive. They work longer hours and/or get more done in less time. Next, look at the processes in your department or organization. Identify one process that could be improved. After you find out all the steps to the existing process, recommend the process improvement idea to your boss. The goal here is simply to develop the mindset of constantly looking for improvements, however small, that will have an impact on the overall operation.

EVALUATE & JOURNAL

On Friday, think about the following questions as you prepare to journal.

1. Describe the process that needed improving and your recommended process improvement. How did that go? Was your idea accepted, or was it referred to someone else?

2. How did it make you feel to view your existing processes in light of continual improvement? Did you feel like you were part of a potential solution, rather than just a part of the process?

3. Do you know anyone at work that excels in this area? What do they do that helps them see below the surface? How do they spot improvement opportunities? What can you learn from that person? How will you adopt this new way of thinking for the future?

Embrace Change.

CONCEPT

President John F. Kennedy once said, "Change is the law of life. And those who look only to the past or present are certain to miss the future." This is an important concept for each of us. Change will happen. Count on it. Oh, we may not like it. We may not agree with it. It doesn't matter. Change will happen anyway. What we can do, however, is be prepared.

First, let's consider some potential sources of change. External sources could include the economy, technology, legislative and regulatory policies, demographics, or foreign competition. Internal sources could include products, suppliers, systems, processes, or the labor market.

"How many of these can I influence or impact?" you may ask. Hardly any of them. But that doesn't mean we cannot, and should not, be personally prepared for change.

The best tool for evaluating one's options is to conduct a SWOT analysis. A SWOT analysis illustrates what to look for in sizing up a company's Strengths, Weaknesses, Opportunities, and Threats. [18] For example, let's say we are a small corner doughnut shop. A typical SWOT analysis would look like this:

Strengths *potential strengths, competitive capabilities*	Weaknesses *potential weaknesses, competitive deficiencies*
• We bake fresh doughnuts every morning • We are located on the main boulevard	• The local grocery started a bakery department • Their donut prices are 5 cents cheaper
Opportunities *potential company opportunities*	Threats *potential external threats to company's well-being*
• We plan to offer drive-through convenience • There is a new metro stop planned next year	• The price of wheat is constantly on the rise • The public wants lower-fat products

The important lesson about change is that we must be prepared. We can't be prepared if we don't have the facts. Once we know where we stand and what to anticipate, we can start looking for options. By anticipating changes in our market, we can get more focused on increasing revenue sources and controlling costs.

APPLICATION

This week, begin to anticipate potential changes in your market. What things are happening locally, nationally, or globally that could have an adverse impact on your organization? If the worst-case scenario happened, how would you and your organization survive? Start asking those questions now. Then, ask those same questions of yourself. What are your strengths? What are your weaknesses? Where do you need to focus your attention to keep yourself marketable? Do a SWOT analysis on yourself, and take a critical look at what skills you bring to the table.

EVALUATE & JOURNAL

On Friday, think about the following questions as you prepare to journal.

1. Were you able to identify at least a few potential threats to your organization? What were they? Have you shared your ideas with your boss?

2. Record your SWOT analysis on yourself.

3. What did you learn from your own SWOT exercise? Did you discover any weaknesses that need your attention? Do you need more training or education? What will you do about it?

4. Finally, are you prepared for change? What can you do today that will make you ready for tomorrow?

Practice, Practice, Practice. Practice Makes Perfect.

CONCEPT

Football coach Vince Lombardi once said, "Practice does not make perfect. Only perfect practice makes perfect." In other words, not just any practice will do, but practicing the important basics is what eventually leads to success.

That makes sense. When you think about it, the difference between a novice and a professional is how well they do the basics. For example, in basketball there are only four basic skills: dribbling, passing, shooting, and rebounding. But, oh, what a difference between a Michael Jordan and a local high school player. In ballet, there are only five basic positions: first, second, third, fourth, and fifth. Again, what a difference between the professional ballerinas in *Swan Lake* and how our daughters perform at a dance class. The point is, once you know the basics, there is nothing more … except practice, practice, practice. It is during practice that we learn the finer points of dribbling and passing or how to do a better plié or relevé.

So, how does this apply to self-management principles? It's the same. According to the U.S. Department of Labor, [19] employers look for people with certain foundational skills: basic reading, writing, speaking, and listening; such thinking skills as the ability to learn, reason, make decisions, and solve problems. Employers also look for such personal qualities as individual responsibility, self-management, sociability, and integrity, just to name a few. Again, it is by practicing these basic skills over and over that great employees are created.

APPLICATION

This week, look at the basics of your job. What are they? Make a list. Now check off the basic skills that you need to practice to get better. Ask yourself, "What would it take for me to become the 'Michael Jordan' of my position?" Identify at least two or three things that you could start practicing today that would help you become an expert at what you do tomorrow.

EVALUATE & JOURNAL

On Friday, think about the following questions as you prepare to journal.

1. With regard to your current job, how did going back to the basics help you identify areas of improvement? What were they?

2. What were the two or three things you decided to practice to perfection? How do you think this will help you in your career success immediately? How about in the future?

3. This is your last journaling exercise. How has journaling helped you make changes in your habits and improvements in your performance?

4. What is the most important thing you learned over the course of these lessons? Which ones were most meaningful for you?

ENDNOTES

1   Ziglar, Zig. *See You at the Top*. Pelican Publishing, Gretna, LA. 1998.

2   Luft, J. *Group Processes: An Introduction to Group Dynamics,* Second Edition. National Press Books, Palo Alto, CA. 1970. Based on *Johari Window: A Graphic Model of Awareness in Interpersonal Relations* (http://www.augsburg.edu/education/edc210/johari.html).

3   Covey, Stephen R. *The 7 Habits of Highly Effective People*. Free Press, NY, NY. 1989.

4   Compiled from the work of John G. Miller, *QBQ: Question Behind the Question*. Penguin Group, NY, NY. 2001.

5   Hagerman, Paul Stirling, *It's a Weird World*. Sterling Publishing Co. Inc, NY, NY. 1990.

6   Taken from Arina Nikitina Goal Setting Guide (http://www.goal-setting-guide.com/overcoming-fear-of-failure.html). 2004.

7   W. Mitchell's official website (http://www.wmitchell.com).

8   Pintrich, Paul R., and Dale H. Schunk. *Motivation in Education*. Prentice Hall, Upper Saddle River, NJ, 2002.

9   Covey, Stephen R. *The 7 Habits of Highly Effective People*. Free Press, NY, NY. 1989.

10 Simeone, Harry. "My Bonnie Lies Over the Ocean." 1947.

11 Covey, Stephen R. *The 7 Habits of Highly Effective People*. Free Press, NY, NY. 1989.

12 Chitwood, Roy. *World Class Selling*. Best Sellers Publishing, Minneapolis, MN. 1996.

13 Rosenberg, Marshall B., Ph.D. *Nonviolent Communication: A Language of Life*. Puddle Dancer Press, Encinitas, CA. 2003.

14 Garlikov, Rick. *The Socratic Method: Teaching by Asking Instead of by Telling* (http://www.garlikov.com/Soc.Meth.html). 2001.

15 Levine, Robert V. *The Power of Persuasion: How We're Bought and Sold*. John Wiley & Sons, Hoboken, NJ. 2003.

16 Shakespeare, William. *The Merchant of Venice* (http://www.allshakespeare.com/quotes/348). 3.1.60-63.

17 Senge, Peter. *The Fifth Discipline,* First Edition. Currency, NY, NY. 1994.

18 Thopson, Arthur A., Jr., and A.J. Strickland, III. *Strategic Management, Concepts and Cases,* 13th Edition. McGraw-Hill, NY, NY, 2003.

19 The Secretary's Commission on Achieving Necessary Skills (http://www.scans.jhu.edu/).

INDEX

52 SECRETS TO BEING

52 SECRETS TO BEING

ABOUT THE AUTHOR

As founder of Power Training Institute, Bonnie Cox offers management and communications training solutions as a corporate facilitator, professional trainer, and motivational speaker. Her custom-designed programs include innovative, interactive exercises to ensure her curriculum has immediate application. As a human resources professional, Bonnie lends more than 20 years of experience in human resources, employment law, training and development, and sales management to her workshops and seminars.

The demand for Bonnie's skills as a professional trainer and consultant has her booked year-round to help top business clients achieve cultural change and organizational growth. She also conducts sales and management training workshops for corporations in diverse lines of business, including banking, aerospace, manufacturing, and distribution.

As Vice President of Training and Development for Select Personnel Services[®], Bonnie is responsible for the company's branch training and career development programs. She established Select University, and intensive and progressive training school specializing in five areas for study: Customer Service, Sales, Operations, and Branch and Regional Management.

Bonnie is also an adjunct professor for UCSB Extension, Antioch University, and Santa Barbara City College's Professional Development Department. She holds a B.S. Degree in Business Management & Finance and has M.A. Degree in Organizational Management.

Bonnie lives in Santa Barbara with her husband, David.